LOW

CALORIE

LOW
CALORIE

OVER 80 DELICIOUS RECIPES

Nutritionist Fiona Hunter
Project Editor Elizabeth Yeates
Senior Designer Vanessa Hamilton
Designer Saskia Janssen
Senior Jacket Creative
Mark Penfound
Pre-Production Producer
Rebecca Fallowfield
Producer Konrad Kirkham
Special Sales Creative
Project Manager Alison Donovan

First published in Great Britain in 2015 by
Dorling Kindersley Limited,
80 Strand, London WC2R 0RL

Material previously published in
The Diabetes Cooking Book (2010),
The Gluten-free Cookbook (2012),
Family Kitchen Cookbook (2013), and
Complete Family Nutrition (2014)

Copyright © 2010, 2012, 2013, 2014, 2015
Dorling Kindersley Limited
A Penguin Random House Company
001 – 284138 – Mar/15

A CIP catalogue record for this book
is available from the British Library.
ISBN 978-0-2412-0085-8

Printed in China

All images © Dorling Kindersley Limited
For further information see: **www.dkimages.com**

A WORLD OF IDEAS:
SEE ALL THERE IS TO KNOW

Contents

Introduction

The food we eat can have an important effect on our health and wellbeing. A healthy diet will help protect against diseases, increase resistance to colds and other infections, boost energy levels, help combat stress, and improve physical and mental performance. Eating well doesn't have to be difficult – you just need to know the key foods to include in your diet.

THE RECIPE FOR A HEALTHY DIET

The three key ingredients in a healthy diet are variety, balance, and moderation.

Variety

Your body needs over 40 different nutrients to accomplish every bodily task. No single food or food group – fruit and vegetables, proteins, carbohydrates, dairy, and fats – can provide all the essential nutrients, which is why you need to choose a variety of foods. The greater the variety of foods in your diet, the more chance you have of getting the key nutrients you need.

Balance

Ensure you eat the right amount of food from all of the food groups (see *Healthy eating in a nutshell*, right). Eating a balanced diet will provide your body with the energy and nutrients it needs. It will also keep your weight within its ideal range.

Moderation

Healthy eating doesn't mean giving up the foods you enjoy, it is simply a question of learning to eat them in moderation. By choosing natural and unprocessed foods and using cooking methods that use little or no fat (steaming and grilling for example), you can still enjoy all your favourite foods.

HEALTHY EATING IN A NUTSHELL

Eat a varied diet containing all of the food groups. Experts recommend the following guidelines:

• **Fruit, vegetables, and plant-based food:** eat plenty of fruit and vegetables and other plant-based foods, such as beans and pulses. You should have at least five portions a day, making up a third of your daily food intake.

• **Protein:** this includes meat, poultry, fish, and eggs. Aim to eat two to three small portions every day and always choose lean cuts of meat, with any excess fat removed.

• **Carbohydrates:** the body needs starchy (also known as complex) carbs to convert into energy. These include potatoes, cereals, and grains, plus bread and pasta. Eat at least five portions a day and choose wholegrains where possible.

• **Dairy:** milk, yogurt, and cheese provide us with essential calcium and other vitamins and minerals. Eat two to three low-fat portions a day.

• **Fats:** these should be eaten in moderation. Some fats are better than others: avoid saturated and trans fats, which are found in processed foods, as they clog arteries with cholesterol. Healthier unsaturated fats (poly- and monounsaturated) can reduce cholesterol levels, so it is always better to eat and use these. They are found in rapeseed oil and avocados.

HOW TO USE THE RECIPES

Icons These appear at the top of every recipe, and advise on preparation and cooking times.

Cook's tip These give useful advice on how to adapt a recipe or how to prepare a certain ingredient.

Nutrition boxes The nutritional breakdown provides the amount of calories, protein, fat, carbohydrates, and sugar per serving.

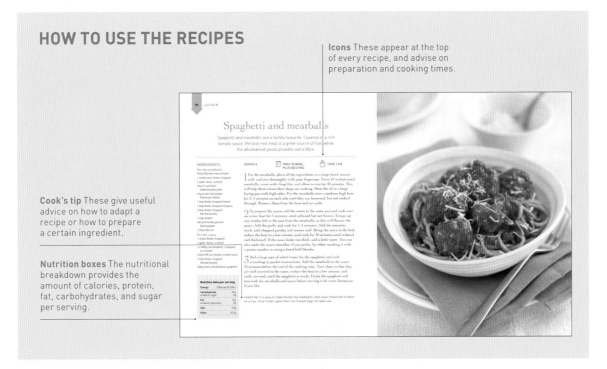

Counting calories

Our bodies need energy in order to function, but we often end up consuming much more than we really need. Calories are the unit used to measure the energy in food and drinks, and are a helpful tool for monitoring your daily energy intake. Unused calories are stored in the body as fat, but if you consume fewer calories than you use, your body burns its fat for fuel and you lose weight.

A CAREFUL BALANCE

Your body needs calories in the same way a car needs fuel. If you drive at an average speed, you won't need as much fuel, whereas if you drive at high speeds, you'll need more fuel. The same applies to your calorie intake.

According to how active you are, the number of calories you need each day depends on your age, gender, and weight. On average, women should aim to consume around 2000 kcals per day, and men 2500 kcals. Kilocalories (abbreviated to kcals) are the most commonly used unit in this country; 1 kcal is equivalent to 1000 calories.

Just a small imbalance between a person's calorie intake and the amount of energy used can lead to slow but steady weight gain. If you want to lose weight you simply need to tip the balance in the other direction, and burn more calories than you consume – this will cause the body to draw on fat reserves for the energy it needs. You can lose weight by restricting the number of calories you eat or increasing the amount of calories you use by being more active. Without doubt, the best way to lose weight is through a combination of diet and exercise. If you're concerned about your weight or calorie intake, consult your GP.

MAKE EVERY CALORIE COUNT

If you are trying to reduce your calorie intake, it's important to make every calorie you eat count, to ensure that you are getting all the essential nutrients you need. The best way to do this is to base your diet around fresh, unprocessed foods. Some foods, particularly those that are high in fat, contain lots of calories, but this doesn't mean you need to avoid them completely, simply that you need to be careful with the amount you eat. Fill up on low calorie foods to satisfy any hunger pangs; a banana is 103 kcals, compared to a cupcake, which is 300 kcals.

HOW LOW SHOULD YOU GO?

Experts have calculated that to lose around 1kg (2lbs) a week you need to reduce your calorie intake by around 500 kcals a day, which means that most women should be able to lose weight on around 1500 kcals day (2000 kcals for men). It's important to spread your calorie allowance throughout the day – eating little and often is the best way to keep blood sugar levels stable and to avoid hunger. Take care not to restrict your calories too severely, as diets that provide fewer than 1200 calories make it difficult to get all the nutrients your body needs to stay healthy.

How much does my body need?

Each individual has different energy needs, so it's important to work out what yours are rather than depending on intake guidelines. Basal metabolic rate (BMR) measures how much energy you need for essential functions such as breathing and heart rate. There are many calculators online that use BMR as a basis for calculating an individual's daily energy needs; NHS advice suggests looking out for calculators that use the Harris-Benedict equation.

MAKE BETTER CHOICES

Choose your snacks carefully. Fruit and vegetables are often more filling than foods with more calories per gram. The below are all 150 kcals.

50g (2oz) cheese = 150g (5½oz) tzatziki, 100g 3½oz carrot, 100g (3½oz) pepper, 75g (2½oz) asparagus

250ml (9floz) apple juice = 2 apples (100g/3½oz each)

BREAKFAST

Muesli breakfast bars

Try baking this modern take on an old-fashioned favourite – the flapjack. Full of slow-release carbohydrates, these muesli breakfast bars make a perfect breakfast-on-the-go when you're in a rush.

INGREDIENTS

115g (4oz) butter, plus extra for greasing

100g (3½oz) light brown sugar

115g (4oz) golden syrup or runny honey

300g (10 oz) rolled oats

100g (3½oz) raisins

50g (1¾oz) mixed nuts, chopped

MAKES 12    **PREP** 15 MINS   **COOK** 30 MINS

1 Preheat the oven to 150°C (300°F/Gas 2). Grease your baking tin. Melt the butter, sugar, and golden syrup or runny honey in a saucepan over a low heat.

2 Measure out the rolled oats, raisins, and mixed nuts and place them into a large mixing bowl. Mix in the melted ingredients from the saucepan, using a wooden spoon to combine them evenly.

3 Spread the mixture evenly in a 30 x 23 x 4cm (12 x 9 x 1½in) baking tin, using a potato masher to help compress the mixture well down in the tin. Bake for 20–30 minutes, or until golden brown.

4 When the mixture is baked, leave it to cool slightly. When cool enough to handle, cut it into 12 squares with a knife, holding the warm tin with a cloth. Take the squares out when they're cold.

Nutrition data per serving

Energy	266kcals/1113kJ
Carbohydrate	36g
of which sugar	21g
Fat	12g
of which saturates	6g
Salt	0.17g
Fibre	2.3g

Tropical breakfast smoothies

Using frozen fruit is an easy way to make this instant healthy smoothie, with no fruit preparation required.

INGREDIENTS

2 bananas
200g (7oz) frozen mango cubes
8 tbsp Greek yogurt
3 tbsp runny honey
500ml (16fl oz) apple juice
ice cubes, to serve (optional)

MAKES 4 GLASSES **PREP 5 MINS**

1 Place all the ingredients in a blender and process until you have a thick, smooth drink. Make sure you only half-fill the blender, to prevent splashes. (You may have to blend your smoothies in batches.)

2 Pour into glasses to serve. Add ice cubes if you like, or if it is a particularly hot day.

Nutrition data per serving

Energy	207kcals/879kJ
Carbohydrate	41g
of which sugar	41g
Fat	3.5g
of which saturates	2g
Salt	trace
Fibre	2.5g

Banana and muesli bread

Packed with wholesome fruits, nuts, and slow-release carbohydrates, a slice of this fruit loaf in the morning will keep you going till lunch.

INGREDIENTS

175g (6oz) wholemeal flour

85g (3oz) sugar-free muesli

125g (4½oz) polyunsaturated margarine

85g (3oz) fructose

2 tsp baking power

¼ tsp ground cinnamon

2 large eggs, beaten

4 ripe bananas, about 350g (12oz), mashed

85g (3oz) pecan nuts, roughly chopped

MAKES 1 LOAF   **PREP** 15 MINS   **COOK** 45-60 MINS

1 Preheat the oven to 160°C (325°F/Gas 3). Grease and line the bottom of a 900g (2lb) loaf tin with non-stick baking parchment.

2 Place the flour, muesli, margarine, fructose, baking powder, cinnamon, and eggs in a large bowl. Beat together until evenly mixed. Stir in the banana and pecan nuts, taking care not to over-mix.

3 Spoon the mixture into the prepared loaf tin and bake for 45 minutes–1 hour, or until the cake looks done and feels springy in the centre. You may need to cover it with foil halfway through cooking if it is browning too quickly. Allow the cake to cool in the tin for 5 minutes, then carefully turn out on to a wire cooling rack.

Nutrition data per serving

Energy	267kcals/1118kJ
Carbohydrate	34g
of which sugar	17g
Fat	13g
of which saturates	3g
Salt	0.5g
Fibre	2.6g

Crunchy muffins

Muffins are easy to make – the method here is very forgiving and allows
a few lumps in the batter – and quick to cook. They are also perfect
for a satisfying breakfast-on-the-go.

INGREDIENTS

300g (10oz) plain flour
1 tbsp baking powder
½ tsp salt
125g (4½oz) granulated sugar
1 egg
2 tbsp vegetable oil
275ml (9fl oz) whole milk
125g (4½oz) raspberries
150g (5½oz) white chocolate,
    finely chopped
85g (3oz) crunchy oat cereal

MAKES 12    **PREP** 30-35 MINS   **COOK** 25 MINS,
PLUS COOLING

1 Preheat the oven to 200°C (400°F/Gas 6). Sift the plain flour, baking
powder, and salt into a mixing bowl, tapping the edges to encourage
it to slip through. Stir in the sugar.

2 Crack the egg into a jug and add the oil. Beat the egg and oil
together with a whisk until they are light and fluffy. Add the
milk and then whisk the mixture until well combined.

3 Fold the egg mixture into the flour mixture. The mixture will
be lumpy but, when you have finished mixing, no flour should
be visible in the batter. Now fold in the raspberries and chocolate.

4 Put 12 paper muffin cases into a 12-hole muffin tray and spoon
the mixture into them, being sure to divide it equally between
the cases. The easiest way is to use a dessertspoon and the back of
a teaspoon.

5 Sprinkle some of the crunchy oat cereal on top of each muffin,
dividing it equally between them. Bake the muffins in the centre
of the hot oven for 25 minutes, or until risen and golden.

6 Remove the muffins from the oven and allow them to cool for
5 minutes in the muffin tray, or until cool enough to handle.
Now carefully transfer each one to a wire rack to cool completely.

Nutrition data per serving

Energy	271kcals/1141kJ
Carbohydrate	37g
of which sugar	21g
Fat	9g
of which saturates	3.5g
Salt	0.7g
Fibre	1.5g

Turkish eggs

This dish, known as "menemen" in Turkey, makes for a spicy and utterly moreish breakfast. Add more chilli if you like it hot.

INGREDIENTS

1 tbsp olive oil

1 onion, sliced

1 green pepper, sliced

1 red pepper, sliced

1 orange pepper, sliced

150g (5½oz) Greek yogurt

3 tbsp chopped mint leaves

2 garlic cloves, crushed

1 red chilli, deseeded and finely chopped

400g can of chopped tomatoes

pinch of caster sugar

salt and freshly ground black pepper

4 eggs

3 tbsp roughly chopped coriander leaves

SERVES 4 PREP 15 MINS  COOK 40-45 MINS

1 Heat the oil in a large, non-stick frying pan over a medium heat and cook the onion for 5 minutes. Add the peppers to the pan and cook for 20 minutes, stirring occasionally.

2 Meanwhile, place the yogurt, mint, and garlic in a small serving bowl and stir together. Cover and set aside.

3 Add the chilli, tomatoes, and sugar to the frying pan, season well, and cook for 10 minutes.

4 Make 4 hollows in the tomato mixture and crack an egg into each. Cover the pan and cook for 5–10 minutes, or until the eggs are cooked to your liking.

5 Sprinkle the dish with the coriander and serve with the herb and garlic yogurt.

Nutrition data per serving	
Energy	208kcals/871kJ
Carbohydrate	13g
of which sugar	13g
Fat	12g
of which saturates	4g
Salt	0.5g
Fibre	4g

Baked eggs with spinach

Easy to put together and very healthy, this manages to
taste far more indulgent than it really is.

INGREDIENTS

30g (1oz) butter, plus extra
    for greasing
350g (12oz) frozen spinach
salt and freshly ground black
    pepper
1/4 tsp grated nutmeg
100g (3½oz) Greek-style yogurt
4 eggs

SERVES 4  **PREP** 15 MINS  **COOK** 20 MINS

1 Preheat the oven to 180°C (350°F/Gas 4). Butter four 150ml (5fl oz)
   ramekins and place on a baking tray.

2 Cook the spinach in a pan, according to the packet instructions.
   Drain well and set aside to cool. Once cooled, squeeze out any
water and chop it finely.

3 Heat the butter in the pan the spinach was cooked in. Add the
   spinach and stir in the seasoning and nutmeg. Remove from the
heat and stir in the yogurt.

4 Divide the creamy spinach between the ramekins and press down
   in the centres to make dips for the eggs to sit in.

5 Carefully break an egg into each ramekin and season well. Bake
   for 15 minutes, or until the eggs are just cooked.

Nutrition data per serving

Energy	198kcals/821kJ
Carbohydrate	2.5g
of which sugar	2.5g
Fat	16g
of which saturates	7.5g
Salt	0.7g
Fibre	2.5g

Mexican scrambled eggs

Eggs are a great source of protein, which helps you to feel full for longer, making this a good choice for breakfast or a light lunch.

INGREDIENTS

2 tbsp vegetable oil

½ red pepper, deseeded and finely diced

4 spring onions, finely chopped

1 small green chilli, deseeded and finely chopped

4 eggs, beaten

salt and freshly ground black pepper

1 tbsp chopped coriander leaves, to serve

SERVES 2   **PREP** 5 MINS   **COOK** 5 MINS

1 Heat the oil in a small, heavy frying pan and add the pepper, spring onion, and chilli. Fry for 2–3 minutes.

2 Pour in the eggs and season to taste. Stir, with a wooden spoon, for 1–2 minutes or until the eggs are scrambled to your liking. Sprinkle with the coriander to serve.

Nutrition data per serving

Energy	292kcals/1214kJ
Carbohydrate	4g
of which sugar	4g
Fat	24g
of which saturates	5g
Salt	0.4g
Fibre	4g

Buckwheat pancakes with orange

The slightly nutty flavour of buckwheat flour combines well with oranges. The secret is to treat the batter gently.

INGREDIENTS

100g (3½oz) buckwheat flour

25g (scant 1oz) rice flour

salt

1 tsp sugar

1 egg, beaten

200ml (7fl oz) milk

3 oranges, peeled and thinly sliced, any juice reserved

1½ tbsp maple syrup, plus extra

sunflower oil, for frying

SERVES 4

 **PREP** 15 MINS, PLUS RESTING

 **COOK** 30 MINS

1 To make the batter, place the flours in a bowl along with a pinch of salt and the sugar, and mix. Make a well in the middle and add the egg. Stir well. Mix the milk and 150ml (5fl oz) water in a jug and gradually pour it into the flour, whisking with a balloon whisk until the batter is smooth and no longer lumpy. Set aside to rest for 30 minutes or overnight in the fridge.

2 For the oranges, heat a griddle pan over a high heat until hot. Mix any reserved orange juice with the maple syrup and brush over the orange slices to coat both sides. Place a few slices at a time on the griddle pan and cook each side for 2 minutes until they take on a little colour. Set aside.

3 Stir the batter. Heat 1 tablespoon oil in a non-stick frying pan or a crêpe pan over a high heat until hot. Swirl it around the pan so it just coats, and tip most of it out into a jug (to reuse). Reduce the heat to low-medium and add a ladleful of batter. Tilt the pan so it spreads; the mixture will be thick so it won't cover the pan completely. Cook for 2 minutes or until the underside is pale golden, then flip it and cook for 2 more minutes. To serve, top with orange slices and a drizzle of maple syrup. Repeat to use up all the batter.

Cook's tip: If freezing, layer the pancakes between greaseproof paper and seal in a freezer bag. To serve, defrost overnight and reheat in a frying pan or microwave.

Nutrition data per serving

Energy	258kcals/1078kJ
Carbohydrate	40g
of which sugar	16g
Fat	8g
of which saturates	2g
Salt	trace
Fibre	3.4g

Banana, yogurt, and honey pancake stack

Try stacking pancakes for a luxurious breakfast treat.
Younger children especially love their sweet fluffiness.

INGREDIENTS

200g (7oz) self-raising flour, sifted
1 tsp baking powder
40g (1¼oz) caster sugar
250ml (8fl oz) whole milk
2 large eggs, lightly beaten
½ tsp vanilla extract
30g (1oz) unsalted butter, melted and cooled, plus extra for frying
200g (7oz) low-fat Greek yogurt
2–3 bananas, sliced
runny honey, to serve

SERVES 6    **PREP** 10 MINS   **COOK** 15-20 MINS

1 Sift the flour and baking powder into a large bowl and add the sugar. In a jug, whisk together the milk, eggs, and vanilla extract. Make a well in the centre of the flour mixture and whisk in the milk mixture, a little at a time, bringing in the flour as you go. Finally, whisk in the cooled, melted butter until the mixture is smooth.

2 Melt a knob of butter in a large, non-stick frying pan. Pour tablespoons of the batter into the pan, leaving space between them for the batter to spread. Each pancake should become about 8–10cm (3¼–4in) in diameter, but don't worry too much.

3 Cook over a medium heat, reducing the heat if they seem to be cooking too fast. Turn the pancakes when small bubbles appear on the surface and pop. Cook for another 1–2 minutes until golden brown and cooked through. Keep warm in a low oven while you make the remaining pancakes.

4 To serve, create a stack of 3 pancakes layered with low-fat Greek yogurt and banana slices. Finish with a drizzle of honey over the top.

Nutrition data per serving

Energy	317kcals/1336kJ
Carbohydrate	40g
of which sugar	17g
Fat	13g
of which saturates	7g
Salt	0.8g
Fibre	2g

Potato pancakes with smoked salmon

Cook extra mashed potato in the week and you'll have the basis of this fabulous weekend brunch dish.

INGREDIENTS

450g (1lb) cooked, cold mashed potato

1 egg, beaten

25g (scant 1oz) plain flour, plus extra for dusting

salt and freshly ground black pepper

2 tbsp olive oil

100g (3½oz) smoked salmon, thinly sliced

4 tbsp soured cream

2 tbsp chopped dill

lemon wedges, to serve

SERVES 4  **PREP** 10 MINS **COOK** 10-15 MINS

1 Place the potato, egg, and flour in a mixing bowl. Season well and stir to combine. Divide into 8 equal portions and, with flour-dusted hands, shape into rounds about 7cm (2¾in) in diameter.

2 Heat the oil in a large, non-stick frying pan over a medium heat. Carefully add the pancakes to the pan. Cook for 10–15 minutes, occasionally turning the pancakes carefully with a fish slice, until they are browned and hot right through.

3 Transfer the pancakes to warmed plates. Top each with smoked salmon, soured cream, and dill. Season well with black pepper and serve with lemon wedges.

Nutrition data per serving	
Energy	288kcals/1199kJ
Carbohydrate	21g
of which sugar	2g
Fat	18g
of which saturates	7g
Salt	0.9g
Fibre	2g

Apple pancake

Making one large pancake instead of individual ones means you'll be able to sit down to eat with the family.

INGREDIENTS

75g (2¹/₂oz) plain flour, sifted

pinch of salt

1 tsp ground cinnamon

120ml (4fl oz) whole milk

3 large eggs, lightly beaten

¹/₂ tsp vanilla extract

30g (1oz) butter

2 apples, peeled, cored, and sliced into thin wedges

1 tsp lemon juice

2 heaped tbsp soft light brown sugar

icing sugar, to serve

SERVES 4-6

 PREP 10 MINS, PLUS RESTING

COOK 15-20 MINS

1 In a bowl, whisk together the flour, salt, and ½ tsp of the cinnamon. Gradually whisk in the milk, then add the eggs and vanilla extract. Cover the bowl with a clean tea towel and set aside to rest for 30 minutes.

2 Preheat the oven to 230°C (450°F/Gas 8). Melt the butter in a 25cm (10in) non-stick, ovenproof frying pan. Fry the apples and the lemon juice over a medium-high heat for 5 minutes, stirring occasionally, until golden brown. Add the sugar and remaining ½ tsp of cinnamon and gently stir, off the heat, until the sugar dissolves.

3 Pour the batter over the apples and transfer to the hot oven. Bake for 15–20 minutes until the pancake is well puffed up and golden brown. It will deflate as it cools.

4 Turn the pancake out onto a warmed plate, so the apples are on top. Dust evenly with icing sugar and serve while piping hot.

Nutrition data per serving	
Energy	280kcals/1166kJ
Carbohydrate	30g
of which sugar	17g
Fat	13g
of which saturates	6g
Salt	0.6g
Fibre	3g

LUNCH

Ribollita

Meaning "reboiled" in Italian, ribollita is a tasty and economical
dish that is based on a traditional Tuscan soup.

INGREDIENTS

100g (3¹/₂oz) dried haricot beans,
 soaked overnight
2 tbsp extra virgin olive oil
50g (1³/₄oz) pancetta cubes
1 celery stick, finely chopped
1 carrot, finely chopped
1 small onion, finely chopped
2 garlic cloves, crushed
2 sprigs of thyme
750ml (1¹/₄ pints) chicken stock
2 handfuls or 100g (3¹/₂oz)
 kale, shredded
sea salt and freshly ground
 black pepper
25g (scant 1oz) finely grated
 Parmesan cheese

SERVES 4    **PREP** 10 MINS,
PLUS SOAKING   **COOK** 2 HRS

1 Rinse the soaked beans and place in a pan with plenty of cold water.
Bring to the boil, skim off any scum, and reduce the heat to a simmer.
Cook the beans for about 1 hour, until softened. Drain and set aside.

2 Heat the olive oil in a separate large saucepan and add the
pancetta. Cook for 2–3 minutes on a medium heat until crispy.
Add the celery, carrot, and onion, then add the garlic and thyme.
Continue to cook for a further 2–3 minutes, until the vegetables are
softened. Pour in the stock and add the drained beans. Simmer the
stew for 30–40 minutes, uncovered, until the beans are very soft.

3 Add the kale, cover, and cook for 5 minutes until the leaves have
wilted. Season to taste, sprinkle with the Parmesan cheese, and
serve with lots of chunks of crusty bread for dipping.

Nutrition data per serving

Energy	206kcals/860kJ
Carbohydrate	15g
of which sugar	4g
Fat	11g
of which saturates	3g
Salt	1.3g
Fibre	8g

Carrot and ginger soup

Unlike most vegetables, which are most nutritious when eaten raw, cooking carrots increases the availability of betacarotene, which the body can convert into vitamin A.

INGREDIENTS

2 tbsp olive oil

1 large onion, peeled and finely chopped

1 clove of garlic, peeled and crushed

5cm (2in) piece of fresh root ginger, peeled and finely chopped

600g (1lb 5oz) carrots, peeled and roughly chopped

750ml (1¼ pints) vegetable stock

zest and juice of 2 large oranges

salt and freshly ground black pepper

spring onions, chopped, to garnish

SERVES 4 **PREP** 15 MINS **COOK** 50 MINS

1 Heat the oil in large non-stick saucepan, add the onion and cook over a medium heat for 3–4 minutes. Add the garlic, ginger, and carrots and continue to cook for a further 5 minutes, stirring occasionally.

2 Add the stock, orange zest and juice, and season to taste with salt and black pepper. Bring to the boil, then reduce the heat, cover, and simmer for 40 minutes or until the carrots are soft.

3 Blend the soup either in a food processor or with a hand-held blender and reheat gently. If the soup is too thick, you can thin it out with a little extra stock or water. Ladle the soup into bowls, garnish with chopped spring onions, and serve.

Nutrition data per serving

Energy	200kcals/836kJ
Carbohydrate	25g
of which sugar	21g
Fat	8g
of which saturates	1.5g
Salt	1.2g
Fibre	5.5g

Butternut squash soup

Make this rich, velvety soup more sophisticated with
a garnish of sage leaves, quickly fried in light oil.

INGREDIENTS

3 tbsp olive oil

1 onion, chopped

1 leek, white part only, chopped

1 celery stick, chopped

500g (1lb 2oz) butternut squash,
cut into 3cm (1in) cubes

750ml (1¼ pints) vegetable
or chicken stock

½ tbsp chopped sage leaves

salt and freshly ground
black pepper

SERVES 4    **PREP** 5 MINS   **COOK** 20 MINS

1 Heat the oil in a large, heavy-based saucepan with a lid. Add the onion, leek, and celery and cook for 5 minutes until they soften, but do not brown.

2 Add the squash, stock, and chopped sage, and season generously with salt and pepper.

3 Bring to the boil, then reduce the heat to a gentle simmer, cover, and cook for 15 minutes until the squash is tender.

4 Blend the soup, either in a food processor or using a hand-held blender, and reheat gently. Check the seasoning and serve.

Nutrition data per serving	
Energy	175kcals/734kJ
Carbohydrate	12g
of which sugar	7g
Fat	8.5g
of which saturates	1g
Salt	0.6g
Fibre	4g

Smoked oyster soup

This sophisticated soup is a perfect starter for a special lunch or dinner party.
No one will realise it's actually quite simple to make.

INGREDIENTS

2 tbsp olive oil

1 onion, finely chopped

2 large white potatoes, approx. 350g (12oz) in total, peeled and roughly chopped

85g can of smoked oysters in sunflower oil, drained and rinsed

1 litre (1¾ pints) fish stock

4 tbsp whipping cream, plus extra to serve

salt and freshly ground black pepper

1 tbsp dry sherry

SERVES 4  **PREP** 10 MINS **COOK** 30 MINS

1 Heat the olive oil in a large, heavy-based saucepan. Fry the onion over a low heat, covered, for 5–7 minutes until it softens.

2 Add the potatoes, smoked oysters, fish stock, and cream, and season. Bring to the boil, then reduce to a simmer, partially cover, and cook for 20–25 minutes, until the potatoes are soft.

3 Blend the soup in a food processor or using a hand-held blender, then pass it through a sieve so that it is completely smooth.

4 Return the soup to the pan and re-heat gently. Add the sherry and serve with a swirl of cream and sprinkling of pepper.

Nutrition data per serving	
Energy	209kcals/869kJ
Carbohydrate	17g
of which sugar	2g
Fat	13g
of which saturates	5g
Salt	2.5g
Fibre	2g

Chicken, vegetable, and noodle soup

Nothing is more comforting than a bowl of chicken soup. Perfect for when you are feeling under the weather, it is light yet tasty, warming, and nourishing.

INGREDIENTS

For the stock

1 onion, peeled and quartered

1 celery stick, roughly chopped

1 large carrot, roughly chopped

2 leeks, green parts only, roughly chopped

¼ tsp black peppercorns

pinch of sea salt

1 bay leaf

sprig of thyme

2 large or 3 medium chicken legs, about 400g (14oz), skinned

For the soup

2 tbsp olive oil

1 onion, finely chopped

1 large carrot, finely chopped

1 celery stick, finely chopped

2 leeks, white parts only, finely chopped

2 garlic cloves, finely chopped

2–3 tbsp finely chopped flat-leaf parsley

salt and freshly ground black pepper

150g (5½oz) egg noodles

SERVES 4    **PREP** 20 MINS   **COOK** 1 HR 30 MINS

1 Place all the ingredients for the stock in a large, heavy-based saucepan and cover with 2 litres (3½ pints) of cold water. Bring to the boil, then reduce to a simmer, and cook uncovered for 1 hour, until the stock is well flavoured and reduced to about 1.5 litres (2¾ pints). The top may need to be skimmed occasionally if foam forms on the surface.

2 Pour the stock through a colander, retaining the liquid, and set aside the cooked chicken to cool. Discard the vegetables. When the chicken is cool enough to handle, separate the meat from the bone, and shred it roughly.

3 For the soup, clean out the saucepan and return it to the heat. Heat the oil, then add the onion, carrot, celery, and leeks and cook over a low heat for 10 minutes, until softened. Do not brown. Add the garlic and cook for 1 minute. Then add the strained stock and the parsley and season well. Bring to the boil, reduce to a low simmer, and cook, uncovered, for 15 minutes.

4 Meanwhile, cook the noodles according to packet instructions. Drain well in a sieve and use a pair of kitchen scissors to snip them across in several places to make them easier to eat.

5 Add the chicken to the soup and cook for 5 more minutes. Then add the cooked noodles and heat thoroughly before serving.

Cook's tip: If you are cooking the egg noodles in advance, rinse them under a cold tap and drain them well. Tossing the noodles in a little oil will help them to stay separate, and not stick together, when they cool.

Nutrition data per serving

Energy	354kcals/1482kJ
Carbohydrate	37g
of which sugar	10g
Fat	12g
of which saturates	2.5g
Salt	0.7g
Fibre	7.5g

Chinese chicken soup with prawn dumplings

If you don't have time to make dumplings, simply chop the prawns and stir them straight into the soup.

INGREDIENTS

2 large chicken breasts, skinless

salt and freshly ground black pepper

5 spring onions, sliced at an angle

5cm (2in) piece of fresh root ginger, peeled and sliced into matchsticks

1–2 tbsp tamari or soy sauce

$^1/_2$–1 red chilli, thinly sliced at an angle

150g (5$^1/_2$oz) shiitake mushrooms, sliced

125g (4$^1/_2$oz) cooked rice

For the dumplings

350g (12oz) prawns, cooked and peeled

5cm (2in) piece of fresh root ginger, peeled and roughly chopped

1 red chilli, deseeded and finely chopped

small handful of coriander leaves, plus extra to garnish

2 tsp nam pla (fish sauce)

2 tbsp cornflour, plus extra for rolling

SERVES 4    **PREP** 20 MINS   **COOK** 50 MINS

1 For the stock, pour 1.5 litres (2¾ pints) of cold water into a large pan and add the chicken breasts and seasoning. Bring to a steady simmer and cook on a low-medium heat, partially covered, for 15–20 minutes until the chicken is cooked. Remove with a slotted spoon and set aside to cool. Strain the stock into a clean pan; you will need about 1.2 litres (2 pints). Shred the chicken and set aside.

2 For the dumplings, place all the ingredients in a food processor, season, and pulse until minced. Scoop up small handfuls and roll into balls; you may need more cornflour. Place the dumplings on a plate and chill in the fridge.

3 Heat the stock over a low-medium heat, add the spring onions, ginger, tamari or soy sauce, chilli, and the mushrooms, and cook for about 20 minutes. Taste and adjust the seasoning as needed.

4 Stir in the rice and shredded chicken and simmer gently for 2 minutes. Add the dumplings, cover, and cook for about 5–8 minutes. Ladle into bowls and top with coriander leaves to serve.

Nutrition data per serving

Energy	250kcals/1047kJ
Carbohydrate	19g
of which sugar	1g
Fat	2g
of which saturates	0.5g
Salt	2.5g
Fibre	0.9g

Warm herring, new potato, and beetroot salad

A modern version of a Swedish main course salad, this is even more delicious served while the potatoes are warm.

INGREDIENTS

400g (14oz) small new potatoes, peeled and halved

salt and freshly ground black pepper

300g tub of marinated herrings

2 tbsp light olive oil

2 tbsp finely chopped dill

2 heaped tsp Dijon mustard

2 Little Gem lettuces, leaves separated (larger ones halved lengthways)

200g (7oz) cooked baby beetroot (not in vinegar)

3 hard-boiled eggs, peeled and quartered

SERVES 4 **PREP** 10 MINS **COOK** 20 MINS

1 Cook the potatoes in a large pan of boiling salted water until they are tender (about 20 minutes, depending on the potato type). Drain and set aside.

2 Meanwhile, make the dressing in a large salad bowl. Whisk together 4 tbsp of the herring marinade, the oil, dill, and mustard, and season well. Reserve 1 tbsp of the dressing.

3 While the potatoes are warm, toss them in the dressing. Gently toss through the fish and lettuce leaves. In a separate bowl, toss the beetroot with the reserved dressing, then decorate the salad with the eggs and beetroot.

Cook's tip: Marinated herrings and beetroot store, chilled, for weeks. Keep some in your fridge to have the basis of this dish.

Nutrition data per serving

Energy	372kcals/1558kJ
Carbohydrate	27g
of which sugar	13g
Fat	19g
of which saturates	2.5g
Salt	2.1g
Fibre	3g

Mixed bean and goat's cheese salad

The mealy beans perfectly complement the rich cheese.

INGREDIENTS

400g tin of butter beans,
    drained and rinsed

400g tin of flageolet beans,
    drained and rinsed

25g (scant 1oz) bunch of chives,
    finely chopped

2 tsp white wine vinegar

1 tbsp fruity olive oil, plus
    extra to serve

1 tbsp fresh thyme leaves

pinch of chilli flakes

salt and freshly ground black
    pepper

50g packet of pea shoots

lemon juice, to season
    (optional)

100g (3½oz) semi-hard
    goat's cheese, broken up
    into pieces

Serrano ham (optional)

SERVES 4  **PREP 10 MINS**

1 Put the beans in a large bowl and add the chives, vinegar, olive oil, thyme, and chilli flakes and stir to combine. Season well with salt and black pepper.

2 Stir through the pea shoots, taste and add a squeeze of lemon if you wish. Transfer to a shallow serving dish and top with the goat's cheese, a drizzle of olive oil and a twist of freshly ground black pepper. If you are a meat eater, you might try a little Serrano ham as an accompaniment.

Cook's tip: If you prefer, you could use a soft goat's cheese and toss it with the beans; it will become almost like a thick, creamy dressing. You can also substitute rocket for the pea shoots.

Nutrition data per serving

Energy	280kcals/1170kJ
Carbohydrate	30g
of which sugar	3g
Fat	11g
of which saturates	5g
Salt	0.2g
Fibre	8.5g

Tabbouleh

This Lebanese speciality of parsley, mint, tomatoes,
and bulgur is refreshing all year round.

. . . .

INGREDIENTS

115g (4oz) bulgur wheat

juice of 2 lemons

75ml (2¹/₂fl oz) extra virgin olive oil

freshly ground black pepper

225g (8oz) flat-leaf parsley, coarse
  stalks discarded

75g (2¹/₂oz) mint leaves

4 spring onions, finely chopped

2 large tomatoes, deseeded
  and diced

1 head of Little Gem lettuce

SERVES 4   **PREP** 20 MINS

1 Put the bulgur wheat in a large bowl, pour over cold water to just
cover, and leave to stand for 15 minutes, or until the wheat has
absorbed all the water and the grains have swollen.

2 Add the lemon juice and olive oil to the wheat, season to taste with
pepper, and stir to mix.

3 Just before serving, finely chop the parsley and mint. Mix the
parsley, mint, spring onions, and tomatoes into the wheat.

4 Arrange the lettuce leaves on a serving plate and spoon the salad
into the leaves to serve.

Nutrition data per serving

Energy	241kcals/1000kJ
Carbohydrate	25g
of which sugar	3g
Fat	14.5g
of which saturates	2g
Salt	trace
Fibre	1g

Panzanella

This classic Italian salad combines torn bread
tossed with fresh tomatoes and basil.

INGREDIENTS

8 slices of good white bread,
   crusts removed
handful of basil leaves, torn
extra virgin olive oil, for drizzling
1–2 tbsp balsamic vinegar
sea salt and freshly ground
   black pepper
5 tomatoes, skinned and roughly
   chopped (see Cook's tip)
handful of pitted black olives

SERVES 4   **PREP** 10 MINS

1 Tear the bread into chunky pieces and sit them in a bowl. Cover with a little cold water and leave to soak for 2 minutes. Remove and squeeze away any excess water, then place in a serving bowl.

2 Add the basil leaves and a drizzle of olive oil. Sprinkle balsamic vinegar to taste, and season well.

3 When ready to serve, add the tomatoes and olives, and toss together well. Season to taste and drizzle over more oil if required.

Cook's tip: Use firm tomatoes for this salad. It's best made in the summer when full-flavoured tomatoes are plentiful.

Nutrition data per serving

Energy	225kcals/953kJ
Carbohydrate	37g
of which sugar	6g
Fat	6g
of which saturates	1g
Salt	1g
Fibre	3.5g

White bean purée, alfalfa, and carrot pitta pockets

A delicious mix of moist softness and crunch makes these
portable pockets ideal to pack for lunch or a picnic.

INGREDIENTS

400g can of cannellini beans,
    drained and rinsed (reserve
    2 tbsp of the liquid)
2 large garlic cloves, crushed
2 heaped tbsp finely chopped
    flat-leaf parsley leaves
1 tbsp olive oil
¼ tsp salt
freshly ground black pepper
2 tbsp lemon juice
4 wholemeal pitta breads
1 large carrot, coarsely grated
50g (1¾oz) alfalfa shoots or
    other shoots

SERVES 4    **PREP** 15 MINS

1 To make the bean purée, put the beans, garlic, parsley, olive oil,
salt, pepper, lemon juice, and 1 tbsp of the bean liquid into a food
processer and process to a rough paste. If it is too thick add a further
1 tbsp of the liquid (but remember this needs to be a thick paste to
hold up well in the pitta bread).

2 Cut each pitta in half and open to make 8 small pockets. Spread
a layer of bean purée on both inside faces of the pockets.

3 Sprinkle a little carrot and alfalfa into each. Serve layered on top
of each other with the stuffing showing, or pack into a container
for transportation.

Nutrition data per serving	
Energy	287kcals/1203kJ
Carbohydrate	45g
of which sugar	6.5g
Fat	5g
of which saturates	0.7g
Salt	1.8g
Fibre	12g

Pulled pork wraps

This is a great way to use up leftovers from a Sunday lunch
in an instantly portable meal.

INGREDIENTS

350g (12oz) cooked pulled pork

2 heaped tbsp good-quality
    barbecue sauce

4 large wraps

4 large Romaine lettuce leaves

½ cucumber, halved, deseeded,
    and finely sliced

3 tbsp soured cream

SERVES 4    **PREP** 10 MINS

1 Shred the pork finely and mix it with the barbecue sauce. Lay the
wraps on a work surface. Flatten the lettuce leaves by pressing down
on the central rib, and put a large lettuce leaf onto each wrap, with the
leaf starting at the edge nearest to you. Layer a line of the sliced
cucumber along the lettuce leaf, about 3cm (1in) thick, and top each
line of cucumber with ½ tbsp of the soured cream.

2 Lay one-quarter of the pork along each line of soured cream. Now
take the remaining soured cream and smear a little, with the back
of a spoon, all over the piece of wrap furthest from you (it should cover
one-third of the wrap). This helps stick it together.

3 Carefully roll up the wrap by picking up the side nearest to you and
folding it over the filling. Continue to roll it away from you until the
wrap bread meets itself and sticks together with the soured cream.
Slice each end off carefully and cut the wraps in half on a diagonal to
serve, or wrap and pack into a container for transportation.

Nutrition data per serving	
Energy	380kcals/1599kJ
Carbohydrate	42g
of which sugar	4g
Fat	9g
of which saturates	3.6g
Salt	0.9g
Fibre	3g

Spice-rubbed salmon

This simple Cajun-inspired rub instantly livens up any fish,
and is ideal for those who can find fish dull.

INGREDIENTS

1 tsp smoked paprika
1 tsp cayenne pepper
1/2 tsp dried thyme
1 tsp soft light brown sugar
1/2 tsp salt
4 skinless salmon fillets, approx.
    150g (5 1/2oz) each
2 tbsp olive oil

SERVES 4    **PREP** 5 MINS,
PLUS RESTING    **COOK** 5-10 MINS

1 Combine the spices, thyme, sugar, and salt in a mortar and pestle
or a spice grinder and grind to a fine powder.

2 Rub the mixture over both sides of the fish, cover with cling film,
and leave to rest in the fridge for 1 hour, so the flavours can sink
into the fish.

3 Preheat the grill on its highest setting and line a grill pan with
foil. Brush the fish with a little oil on both sides, being careful not to
dislodge the spice rub, and grill for 3–4 minutes on each side, depending
on thickness. Serve with a green salad and a little steamed rice.

Nutrition data per serving	
Energy	324kcals/1384kJ
Carbohydrate	1g
of which sugar	1g
Fat	22g
of which saturates	3.5g
Salt	0.6g
Fibre	0g

Falafel

Based on chickpeas, these tasty and substantial
bites are a Middle Eastern classic.

INGREDIENTS

225g (8oz) dried chickpeas,
    soaked overnight in
    cold water
1 tbsp tahini
1 garlic clove, crushed
1 tsp salt
1 tsp ground cumin
1 tsp turmeric
1 tsp ground coriander
$^{1}/_{2}$ tsp cayenne pepper
2 tbsp finely chopped parsley
juice of 1 small lemon
vegetable oil, for frying

SERVES 4   **PREP** 25 MINS, PLUS
SOAKING AND CHILLING   **COOK** 15 MINS

1 Drain the soaked chickpeas and place them in a food processor with the
rest of the ingredients. Process until finely chopped but not puréed.

2 Transfer the mixture to a bowl and set it aside for at least 30 minutes
(and up to 8 hours), covered in the refrigerator.

3 Wet your hands and shape the mixture into 12 balls. Press the tops
down slightly to flatten.

4 Heat 5cm (2in) of oil in a deep pan or wok. Fry the balls in batches
for 3–4 minutes, or until lightly golden. Drain on kitchen paper and
serve. A simple green salad makes a good accompaniment.

Nutrition data per serving

Energy	277kcals/1161kJ
Carbohydrate	30g
of which sugar	1.5g
Fat	13.5g
of which saturates	1.5g
Salt	1g
Fibre	6g

Noodles with mushrooms and sesame seeds

These rich-tasting Japanese noodles work perfectly with woody mushrooms and crisp sugarsnap peas.

INGREDIENTS

1 tbsp sunflower oil

1 onion, sliced

3 garlic cloves, sliced

200g (7oz) sugarsnap peas

salt and freshly ground
  black pepper

250g (9oz) chestnut
  mushrooms, quartered

120ml (4fl oz) vegetable stock

175g (6oz) soba wheat noodles
  with buckwheat

2 tbsp sesame seeds

2 tbsp fresh basil leaves, torn

SERVES 4 **PREP** 5 MINS **COOK** 20 MINS

1 Heat the oil in a wok, add the onion and cook for about 5 minutes until soft and translucent. Add the garlic and stir for a few seconds, then add the sugarsnap peas and stir-fry for a further 5 minutes, moving the ingredients all the time so that the garlic doesn't burn. Season well with salt and black pepper.

2 Add the mushrooms, stir to coat, and cook for a few minutes until they begin to soften. Pour in the stock, a little at a time, and bring to the boil. Reduce to a simmer and cook for a couple of minutes.

3 Meanwhile, cook the noodles in a pan of salted boiling water for 5–7 minutes, then drain well.

4 Stir the noodles into the mushrooms. Sprinkle with sesame seeds and stir in the basil leaves.

Nutrition data per serving

Energy	270kcals/1123kJ
Carbohydrate	41g
of which sugar	4g
Fat	8g
of which saturates	1g
Salt	1g
Fibre	2.5g

Sweet potato, red onion, and thyme galettes with chilli

A shop-bought all-butter puff pastry is a great time saver, and all but indistinguishable from home-made pastry.

INGREDIENTS

MAKES 6    PREP 20 MINS   COOK 50 MINS

For the filling

2 sweet potatoes, approx. 300g (10oz) peeled weight, cut into 1cm (½in) cubes

2 red onions, cut into 1cm (½in) cubes

1 tbsp olive oil

salt and freshly ground black pepper

½ red chilli, deseeded and finely chopped

1 tsp finely chopped thyme leaves

For the pastry

375g (12oz) ready-made puff pastry

plain flour, for dusting

1 egg yolk, beaten

1 Preheat the oven to 200°C (400°F/Gas 6). Toss the sweet potatoes and red onions in the oil in a large bowl, and season well with salt and pepper. Turn the vegetables out onto a baking tray and bake for 30 minutes until softened and golden at the edges.

2 Roll out the puff pastry on a lightly floured surface into a square about 30 x 40cm (12 x 16in) and cut it into quarters. Lay the pastry rectangles on baking trays. Brush them with the egg yolk.

3 Toss the cooked vegetables with the chilli and thyme, and divide equally between the pastries. Spread the vegetables out, leaving a 1cm (½in) clear border to each pastry.

4 Bake for 20 minutes, or until the pastry is puffed up and golden brown at the edges, and the bases are firm to the touch. The pastries are best eaten hot, but set aside to cool for 5 minutes before serving with a leafy green salad.

Nutrition data per serving

Energy	317kcals/1329kJ
Carbohydrate	34g
of which sugar	5g
Fat	18g
of which saturates	8g
Salt	0.6g
Fibre	3.5g

Oven-baked red pepper and tomato frittata

An easy way to cook this simple vegetable and egg dish.

INGREDIENTS

1 tbsp olive oil

1 onion, finely chopped

2 red peppers, deseeded and finely chopped or sliced

salt and freshly ground black pepper

pinch of paprika

4 tomatoes, skinned, deseeded, and flesh chopped

25g (scant 1oz) bunch of chives, finely chopped

4 large eggs, lightly beaten

SERVES 2    **PREP** 15 MINS    **COOK** 30 MINS

1 Preheat the oven to 180°C (350°F/Gas 4). Heat the oil in a medium non-stick frying pan, add the onion and red peppers, and cook for 5–8 minutes until soft. Season with salt and pepper, add the paprika, and stir.

2 Transfer the cooked vegetables to a heatproof dish and stir in the tomatoes and chives. Add the eggs and mix gently, then place in the oven for 20–30 minutes until risen and golden.

3 Allow to cool for a few minutes before serving. A simple green salad makes a good accompaniment.

Cook's tip: Swap herbs to suit the seasons and add a pinch of chilli flakes to heat things up.

Nutrition data per serving

Energy	336kcals/1402kJ
Carbohydrate	22g
of which sugar	19g
Fat	20g
of which saturates	5g
Salt	0.3g
Fibre	0.5g

Farfalle with fresh tomatoes and avocado

A really simple dish – a fresh-tasting no-cook
sauce tossed with pasta bows.

INGREDIENTS

5 tomatoes, diced

1 avocado, halved, stoned
and diced

juice of 1 lemon

salt and freshly ground
black pepper

3 tbsp olive oil

350g (12oz) dried
farfalle pasta

75g (2½oz) wild
rocket leaves

SERVES 4    **PREP** 10 MINS   **COOK** 15 MINS

1 Place the tomatoes in a bowl with the avocado and lemon juice and
season well with salt and pepper. Gently stir to combine, then add
the olive oil and stir again. Set aside to allow the flavours to develop.

2 Meanwhile, cook the pasta in a large pan of boiling salted water
for 10–12 minutes or according to packet instructions. Drain,
return to the pan, and stir in the tomato mixture. Add the rocket
leaves and serve straight away.

Nutrition data per serving

Energy	387kcals/1628kJ
Carbohydrate	52g
of which sugar	5.5g
Fat	17g
of which saturates	3g
Salt	trace
Fibre	4.5g

Pasta salad with prawns and pesto

Home-made pesto takes just minutes to prepare and the flavour
is far superior to shop-bought varieties.

INGREDIENTS

salt and freshly ground
  black pepper
200g (7oz) dried pasta, such as fusilli
60g (2oz) basil leaves
25g (scant 1oz) toasted pine nuts
25g (scant 1oz) grated Parmesan
2 garlic cloves, roughly chopped
80ml (2¾fl oz) extra virgin olive oil
finely grated zest of 1 lemon, plus
  1 tbsp lemon juice
250g (9oz) cooked, peeled
  king prawns

SERVES 4 **PREP** 20 MINS **COOK** 10-12 MINS

1 Bring a large pan of salted water to the boil and cook the pasta according to the packet instructions. Drain and rinse under cold running water until the pasta is cold. Drain well and set aside.

2 Place the basil, pine nuts, Parmesan cheese, garlic, oil, and lemon zest and juice in a food processor and pulse until well blended.

3 Place the pasta in a large serving bowl and stir in the pesto. Season well with pepper and stir to combine. Carefully stir in the prawns.

Nutrition data per serving	
Energy	420kcals/1759kJ
Carbohydrate	36g
of which sugar	1.5g
Fat	22g
of which saturates	4g
Salt	1g
Fibre	2.5g

Tuna patties

These simple fishcakes are so easy to make, especially
if you have some leftover mashed potato.

INGREDIENTS

200g can tuna in spring
water, drained

450g (1lb) cooked, cooled
mashed potato

6 spring onions, very
finely chopped

2 tbsp chopped flat-leaf
parsley leaves

salt and freshly ground
black pepper

1–2 tbsp olive oil

green beans and lemon
wedges, to serve

MAKES 8    **PREP** 15 MINS,
PLUS COOLING    **COOK** 10 MINS

1 Place all the ingredients, except the oil, in a bowl and stir well
to combine. Divide into 8 portions. Shape each portion into an
8cm (3in) round patty.

2 Heat the oil in a large, non-stick frying pan over a medium heat
and cook the patties for 5 minutes on each side. (You may need to
do this in batches; if so, keep them warm while you fry the rest, adding
more oil if needed.) Transfer to warmed plates and serve with green
beans and lemon wedges.

Nutrition data per serving	
Energy	97kcals/407kJ
Carbohydrate	8g
of which sugar	0.7g
Fat	4g
of which saturates	1.5g
Salt	0.1g
Fibre	1g

Mixed bean burger

Vegetarian burgers with a hint of Indian spice.

INGREDIENTS

1 red onion, roughly chopped

2 garlic cloves, finely chopped

1 green chilli, deseeded and roughly chopped

pinch of garam masala

handful of fresh coriander

2 x 400g cans of mixed beans, drained

125g (4½oz) mushrooms, grated

salt and freshly ground black pepper

2 tbsp fresh breadcrumbs

1–2 eggs, lightly beaten

2 tbsp sunflower oil

SERVES 4　　**PREP** 10 MINS, PLUS CHILLING　　**COOK** 15 MINS

1 Place the onion, garlic, chilli, garam masala, coriander, beans, and mushrooms in a food processor and whiz until well combined, but do not overblend and let it become mushy.

2 Season well with salt and black pepper then tip in the breadcrumbs and a little of the egg and pulse until it all binds together but is neither too wet nor too dry – add a little more egg if needed. Shape into 8 patties, arrange on a plate and transfer to the refrigerator for 20 minutes to firm up.

3 Heat the oil in a non-stick frying pan and cook a few burgers at a time for 6–7 minutes or until the underside starts to brown. Turn over the burgers using a fish slice and cook the other side for the same amount of time, adding more oil if needed. You could serve these in wholemeal bread rolls, each with a small quantity of tomato salad.

Nutrition data per serving

Energy	250kcals/1061kJ
Carbohydrate	37g
of which sugar	4g
Fat	5g
of which saturates	1g
Salt	0.3g
Fibre	12g

Potato and thyme rösti with mushrooms

This traditional Swiss favourite never fails to please.

INGREDIENTS

550g (1¼lb) potatoes (use large waxy ones), unpeeled

salt and freshly ground black pepper

few stalks of fresh thyme, leaves only

1 onion, finely chopped

2 tbsp sunflower oil

150g (5½oz) chestnut mushrooms, sliced

2 garlic cloves, finely chopped

SERVES 4    **PREP** 15 MINS   **COOK** 25 MINS

1 Cook the potatoes in a large pan of salted water for 10–15 minutes until just beginning to soften. Remove with a slotted spoon and set aside until cool enough to handle. Grate the potatoes into a bowl and season with plenty of salt and black pepper. Add the thyme and onion, and stir gently.

2 Put 1 tablespoon of the oil into a medium-sized, nonstick frying pan and add the potato mixture, pressing it down so that it becomes a cake – it should be about 1cm (½in) thick. Cook over a low heat for 10–12 minutes until the underside begins to turn golden and form a crust. Invert the cake onto a large plate and return it to the pan to cook the other side until golden. (Alternatively, if the handle of the pan is heatproof, you could finish it off in an oven preheated to a medium heat.)

3 Meanwhile, heat the remaining oil in another frying pan, add the mushrooms and cook for 5 minutes or until they begin to release their juices. Add the garlic and cook for a further couple of minutes, then season to taste. Using a spatula, slide the rösti out of the pan and onto a serving plate. Top with the mushrooms and slice the rösti to serve.

Cook's tip: You can use grated raw potato if you prefer, but do make sure you squeeze out all the water or else the rösti will become wet. You will also need to use a lower heat and cook it for longer, otherwise the inside will not cook.

Nutrition data per serving

Energy	166kcals/699kJ
Carbohydrate	26g
of which sugar	2g
Fat	6g
of which saturates	0.7g
Salt	trace
Fibre	2.6g

Sweet potato cakes

Spring onion adds a crunchy texture to these cakes.

INGREDIENTS

500g (1lb 2oz) cooked sweet potato, mashed (see Cook's tip)

5cm (2in) piece of fresh ginger, peeled and grated

bunch of spring onions, finely chopped

pinch of freshly grated nutmeg

2 eggs, lightly beaten

flour for dusting

3–4 tbsp polenta

vegetable oil for shallow frying

lime wedges, to serve

SERVES 4   **PREP** 10 MINS   **COOK** 20 MINS

1 Place the sweet potato in a large bowl. Add the ginger, spring onions, and nutmeg, then add a little of the egg, a drop at time, reserving plenty for coating, until the mixture binds together.

2 Season well with salt and black pepper, then scoop up a handful of the mixture, roll into a ball, then flatten out into a cake. Repeat until all the mixture is used.

3 Dust the cakes in flour, dip in the reserved egg, then lightly coat with polenta. Heat the oil in a non-stick frying pan and add the cakes a couple at a time. Cook for 2–3 minutes or until the underside turns golden, then carefully flip and cook for a further 2–3 minutes, or until evenly golden brown. Serve with lime wedges for squeezing over.

Cook's tip: To cook the sweet potatoes, you could bake or microwave them, then scoop out the insides and mash with a fork. Alternatively, peel them, cut into chunks, boil, and drain before mashing.

Nutrition data per serving

Energy	272kcals/1140kJ
Carbohydrate	36g
of which sugar	16g
Fat	12g
of which saturates	2g
Salt	0.2g
Fibre	3.5g

DINNER

Fisherman's pie

Haddock is the fish of choice in this traditional family dish,
though you can use other sustainable white fish too.

INGREDIENTS

For the topping

625g (1lb 5oz) potatoes, peeled
and cut into chunks

salt and freshly ground
black pepper

4 tbsp whole milk

60g (2oz) butter

For the filling

3 eggs

1 litre (1¾ pints) whole milk

10 peppercorns

2 bay leaves

1 small onion, quartered

750g (1lb 10oz) skinless haddock
fillets, cut into pieces

90g (3oz) butter

60g (2oz) plain flour

handful of parsley
leaves, chopped

125g (4½oz) cooked prawns,
shelled and deveined

SERVES 6   **PREP** 20 MINS,
                    PLUS INFUSING   **COOK** 50 MINS–1 HR

1 Cook the potatoes in a saucepan of boiling salted water for 15–20 minutes until tender, adding the eggs for the filling for the last 10 minutes. Drain thoroughly. Cool the eggs, then peel, quarter, and set aside. Return the potato to the pan and mash. Heat the milk in a small pan, add the butter, salt and pepper, and stir. Pour the milk mixture into the potatoes and beat over a medium heat for 2 minutes, until fluffy. Taste for seasoning. Set aside.

2 Meanwhile, for the filling, pour the milk into a sauté pan, then add the peppercorns, bay leaves, and onion. Bring to the boil, then remove from the heat, cover, and leave to infuse for 10 minutes.

3 Return the infused milk to the boil, then reduce the heat to low. Add the fish, cover, and simmer for 5–10 minutes, depending on thickness: it should flake easily. Transfer the fish to a large plate, using a slotted spoon; reserve the liquid. Flake the fish.

4 Melt the butter in a pan over a medium heat. Whisk in the flour and cook for 1 minute. Off the heat, gradually add the fish cooking liquid, whisking. Return to the heat and whisk until the sauce boils and thickens. Season and simmer for 2 minutes, then add the parsley.

5 Preheat the oven to 180°C (350°F/Gas 4). Ladle one-third of the sauce into a 2-litre (3½-pint) pie dish. Spoon the flaked fish on top, in an even layer. Cover with the remaining sauce, then scatter with the prawns and quartered eggs, pushing them into the sauce.

6 Spread the mashed potatoes on top to cover the filling, forking it to make an attractive pattern. Bake for 20–30 minutes until brown and bubbling.

Nutrition data per serving

Energy	543kcals/2269kJ
Carbohydrate	32.5g
of which sugar	9g
Fat	30g
of which saturates	16g
Salt	1.1g
Fibre	2.5g

Hake in green sauce

Add extra vegetables, such as lightly cooked peas or asparagus tips,
to the sauce in keeping with its green theme.

INGREDIENTS

2 tbsp olive oil

2 garlic cloves, finely chopped

2 tbsp plain flour

150ml (5fl oz) dry white wine

175ml (6fl oz) fish stock

4 tbsp chopped flat-leaf
parsley leaves

salt and freshly ground
black pepper

4 skin-on hake fillets, approx.
150g (5½oz) each

sautéed potatoes and green
beans, to serve

SERVES 4    **PREP 10 MINS**   **COOK 14-16 MINS**

1 Heat the oil in a large, non-stick frying pan over a medium heat.
Gently fry the garlic for 1 minute.

2 Sprinkle the flour into the pan and stir thoroughly with a wooden
spoon. Cook for 2 minutes, stirring until smooth. Gradually add
the wine, followed by the stock, stirring constantly.

3 Stir in the parsley and simmer very gently over a low heat for
about 5 minutes.

4 Season the fish and add to the pan, skin-side down. Spoon some
sauce over and cook for 2–3 minutes. Turn and cook for a further
2–3 minutes, or until cooked through.

5 Transfer to warmed plates and serve immediately with sautéed
potatoes and green beans.

Nutrition data per serving

Energy	238kcals/998kJ
Carbohydrate	6g
of which sugar	0.3g
Fat	9g
of which saturates	1.5g
Salt	0.8g
Fibre	0.3g

Smoked haddock fishcakes

Try to find Japanese panko breadcrumbs if you can. They give a
wonderful, extra-crispy finish to any fried food.

INGREDIENTS

400g (14oz) potatoes,
    peeled weight

salt and freshly ground
    black pepper

2 tbsp butter

1 tbsp olive oil

1 leek, finely chopped

400g (14oz) skinless smoked
    haddock, undyed if possible

4 tbsp finely chopped flat-leaf
    parsley leaves

finely grated zest of 1 lemon

1 heaped tbsp capers, rinsed,
    dried, and roughly chopped

50g (1¾oz) plain flour

1 egg, lightly beaten

75g (2½oz) panko breadcrumbs
    or day-old breadcrumbs

sunflower oil, for frying

SERVES 4

PREP 40 MINS, PLUS CHILLING

 **COOK 10 MINS**

1 Chop the potatoes into large cubes and put them in a large pan of cold salted water. Bring them to the boil, reduce the heat to a simmer, and cook for 20–25 minutes until soft. (The time will vary depending on the type of potato you use.) When they are cooked, drain and mash them with the butter and plenty of salt and pepper until smooth, but still quite dry and stiff.

2 Meanwhile, heat the oil in a frying pan and gently cook the leek for 5 minutes, until softened, but not browned. Work it into the potato. Set aside to cool completely.

3 At the same time, bring a large saucepan of water to the boil, then add the smoked haddock and reduce the heat to a simmer. Cook gently for 5–7 minutes (depending on thickness), until the fish flakes easily with a fork. Drain the fish and, when it is cool enough to handle, break it into large flakes with your fingers, removing any bones at the same time. Set aside to cool completely.

4 Once the potato and fish have cooled, combine them in a large bowl and add the parsley, lemon zest, and capers. Mix well, being careful not to break up the fish too much, and check for seasoning. Shape the mixture into eight fishcakes, cover, and rest for 30 minutes in the fridge.

5 Prepare 3 shallow bowls, the first with the flour, seasoned well, the next with the egg, and the last with the breadcrumbs. Dip the fishcakes in the flour, patting off excess, then in the egg, then in the breadcrumbs, being sure they are well coated. Cover and rest again in the fridge for a further 30 minutes.

6 Heat 2 large frying pans and add enough sunflower oil to cover the base of each. Fry over a medium heat for 4–5 minutes on each side, until crisp, golden, and heated through.

Nutrition data per serving	
Energy	423kcals/1779kJ
Carbohydrate	39.5g
of which sugar	2g
Fat	17.5g
of which saturates	5.5g
Salt	2.7g
Fibre	3.5g

Mackerel teriyaki

This Japanese-style mackerel is an affordable, tasty way
to enjoy a fish high in healthy omega-3 fatty acids.

INGREDIENTS

2 garlic cloves, finely chopped

2cm (³/₄in) piece of fresh
root ginger, finely chopped

2 tbsp caster sugar

4 tbsp rice vinegar

4 tbsp mirin

4 tbsp sake

4 tbsp soy sauce

salt and freshly ground
black pepper

4 mackerel fillets, approx.
100g (3¹/₂oz) each

1 tbsp vegetable oil

chopped spring onions,
to garnish

noodles and stir-fried
vegetables, to serve

SERVES 4   **PREP** 5 MINS   **COOK** 15 MINS

1 Place the garlic, ginger, sugar, vinegar, mirin, sake, and soy sauce in a small pan and bring to the boil. Reduce the heat and simmer for about 10 minutes, until the mixture has thickened to a coating consistency.

2 Season the fish on both sides. Heat the oil in a large, non-stick frying pan over a medium heat, add the mackerel skin-side down, and cook for 2 minutes until crisp.

3 Turn the fish over and cook for 1 minute. Add the sauce to the pan and cook for 2 minutes more.

4 Place the mackerel on serving plates, drizzle with a little of the sauce, and garnish with the spring onions. Serve with stir-fried vegetables and a small amount of noodles.

Nutrition data per serving

Energy	317kcals/1320kJ
Carbohydrate	9g
of which sugar	9g
Fat	19g
of which saturates	3.5g
Salt	2.8g
Fibre	0g

Spinach and coconut prawn curry

This mild, creamy curry flavoured with coconut makes a light
and fragrant supper dish that is easy to prepare.

INGREDIENTS

2 tbsp sunflower oil

2 red onions, finely chopped

4 garlic cloves, finely chopped

5cm (2in) piece of fresh root
ginger, finely grated

$\frac{1}{4}$–$\frac{1}{2}$ tsp chilli powder

$\frac{1}{2}$ tsp turmeric

2 tsp ground cumin

1 tsp ground coriander

4 large tomatoes, skinned and
finely chopped

400ml (14fl oz) coconut milk

10 fresh or dried curry
leaves (optional)

150g (5$\frac{1}{2}$oz) spinach, shredded

400g (14oz) raw king prawns,
shelled and deveined

$\frac{1}{2}$ tsp caster sugar

salt

plain boiled rice, a small
naan bread, and lime
wedges, to serve

SERVES 4 **PREP** 15 MINS **COOK** 20 MINS

1 Heat the oil in a large, deep-sided frying pan or wok. Add the onions, garlic, and ginger and cook for 2–3 minutes over a low heat until softened. Add the spices and cook for a further 1 or 2 minutes.

2 Add the tomatoes and continue to cook over a low heat for another 2 minutes, until the tomato flesh starts to break down. Add the coconut milk and curry leaves (if using), and bring to the boil. Mix in the spinach and reduce the heat, continuing to cook until the spinach has wilted.

3 Add the prawns, sugar, and a pinch of salt, and cook for a further 2 minutes over a high heat, or until the prawns turn a bright pink colour. Serve with plain boiled rice, a small naan bread, and lime wedges to squeeze over.

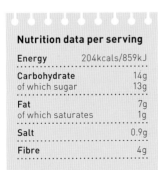

Nutrition data per serving	
Energy	204kcals/859kJ
Carbohydrate	14g
of which sugar	13g
Fat	7g
of which saturates	1g
Salt	0.9g
Fibre	4g

Chicken and broccoli simmered in soy and star anise

Deeply aromatic, this is a great recipe to cook for minimum fuss and very little washing up.

INGREDIENTS

100ml (3¹/₂fl oz) rice wine or dry sherry

3¹/₂ tbsp soy sauce

400ml (14fl oz) chicken stock

4cm (1¹/₂in) fresh root ginger, cut into matchsticks

2 garlic cloves, sliced

4 star anise

3 tbsp soft light brown sugar

4 skinless and boneless chicken breasts

1 tbsp cornflour

150g (5¹/₂oz) sprouting broccoli spears or broccoli florets

SERVES 4    **PREP** 10 MINS   **COOK** 20-25 MINS

1 In a large, deep-sided frying pan or wok, mix the rice wine, soy sauce, stock, ginger, garlic, star anise, and sugar, and bring to the boil over a medium heat. Reduce the heat and simmer for 5 minutes.

2 Add the chicken in a single layer, making sure it is submerged as much as possible, and poach for 7–10 minutes, turning occasionally, until firm. Remove with a slotted spoon, cover, and keep warm.

3 Strain the liquid through a sieve and return it to the pan. Return it to the boil over a medium heat, then reduce the heat to a simmer. Mix the cornflour with 1 tbsp of water and add, whisking until it thickens. Add the broccoli and cook for 3–5 minutes until tender.

4 Pour the sauce over the chicken and arrange the broccoli around to serve.

Nutrition data per serving	
Energy	282kcals/1192kJ
Carbohydrate	16g
of which sugar	12.5g
Fat	2g
of which saturates	0.5g
Salt	2.8g
Fibre	1.5g

Steak glazed with mustard and brown sugar

If you have a kitchen blowtorch, now is the perfect time to use it!
This is a special occasion dish.

INGREDIENTS

4 x 100–150g (3¹/₂–5¹/₂oz) steaks,
    preferably fillet, approx. 3cm (1in)
    thick, at room temperature
1 tbsp olive oil
salt and freshly ground
    black pepper
1 tbsp Dijon mustard
1 tbsp soft light brown sugar

SERVES 4    **PREP 5 MINS**   **COOK 10 MINS**

1 Rub the steaks with the oil and season well with salt and pepper. Fry or chargrill over a high heat until cooked as you like. For rare, allow 2–3 minutes each side; for medium, 3–4 minutes each side; and for well done, 4–5 minutes each side. Allow the meat to rest for about 5 minutes, loosely covered with foil to keep warm.

2 Meanwhile, preheat the grill on its highest setting. Brush each steak on its upper side with a thin layer of mustard, then sprinkle with an even layer of the sugar.

3 Grill the steaks for a minute or 2 only, until the sugar has melted and caramelized over the top. You don't want to cook them any further, just enough to create a great glazed effect.

Nutrition data per serving	
Energy	184kcals/767kJ
Carbohydrate	4g
of which sugar	4g
Fat	9g
of which saturates	3g
Salt	0.4g
Fibre	0g

Chicken and barley stew

A nutritious, warming, and comforting one-pot dish that needs
nothing more than mashed potato on the side.

INGREDIENTS

150g (5½oz) pearl barley
4 tbsp sunflower oil
1 large onion, chopped
1 leek, sliced into 1cm (½in) rings
1 celery stick, cut into
   2cm (¾in) pieces
2 large carrots, cut into
   2cm (¾in) pieces
1 parsnip, cut into 2cm (¾in) pieces
salt and freshly ground
   black pepper
1 tbsp plain flour
8 skinless bone-in chicken thighs
600ml (1 pint) chicken stock
1 bouquet garni

SERVES 4    **PREP** 10 MINS   **COOK** 1 HR 15 MINS

1 Put the barley in a saucepan and cover it with cold water. Place
over a high heat and bring to the boil. Cook for 10 minutes,
skimming off scum. Drain and rinse.

2 In a large flameproof casserole, or heavy-based saucepan with a lid,
heat 2 tbsp of the sunflower oil. Fry the onion, leek, celery, carrots,
and parsnip for 10 minutes over a medium heat until they colour at the
edges. Remove from the pan and wipe it out with kitchen paper.

3 Heat the remaining 2 tbsp of oil in the pan. Season the flour.
Dust the chicken with the flour, shaking off excess. Fry the pieces,
spaced well apart, for 3–5 minutes each side until golden. You may
need to cook in batches. Set aside.

4 Pour in the stock, scraping up the residue from the pan. Return
the vegetables, barley, and chicken. Add the bouquet garni.

5 Bring to the boil, then reduce the heat to a gentle simmer and
cook, covered, for about 45 minutes, until the chicken is cooked
through. Remove the bouquet garni before serving.

Nutrition data per serving

Energy	513kcals/2156kJ
Carbohydrate	45g
of which sugar	10g
Fat	17g
of which saturates	3g
Salt	0.8g
Fibre	6g

Moroccan-spiced chicken

A gently spiced stew, sweet with squash and dried apricots, this
is particularly appealing to younger children.

INGREDIENTS

1 heaped tbsp plain flour

salt and freshly ground
    black pepper

8 skinless bone-in chicken pieces,
    thighs, drumsticks, or a mixture

4 tbsp olive oil

1 large onion, finely chopped

1 red pepper, sliced

1 yellow pepper, sliced

2 garlic cloves, roughly chopped

1 tsp ground cumin

½ tsp ground coriander

½ tsp ground cinnamon

1 tsp smoked paprika

1 tsp dried thyme

400g can chopped tomatoes

500ml (16fl oz) chicken stock

1 tbsp runny honey

250g (9oz) butternut squash, peeled
    and cut into 2cm (¾in) cubes

50g (1¾oz) dried apricots,
    roughly chopped

handful of coriander leaves,
    roughly chopped

SERVES 4    **PREP** 15 MINS    **COOK** 1 HR 10 MINS

1 Place the flour in a freezer bag and season it well. Toss the chicken
in the bag until well coated. Tip out into a sieve and shake to
remove excess flour.

2 Heat 2 tbsp of the oil over a medium heat in a large, heavy-based
saucepan with a lid. Fry the chicken (you may need to do this
in batches), spaced well apart, for 3–5 minutes each side, until golden
brown all over. Set aside while you cook the remaining pieces.

3 Heat the remaining 2 tbsp of oil in the pan and cook the onion,
peppers, and garlic for 3–5 minutes until softened, but not brown.
Add all the spices and the thyme and fry for 1 or 2 minutes until they
release all their fragrances. Add the tomatoes, stock, and honey, and
season to taste.

4 Return the chicken and bring to the boil. Reduce the heat to
a low simmer and cook, covered, for 20 minutes. Add the squash
and apricots and cook, covered, for a further 20 minutes, stirring
occasionally, until the chicken is cooked through. Stir in the
coriander leaves to serve.

Nutrition data per serving

Energy	414kcals/1739kJ
Carbohydrate	26g
of which sugar	20g
Fat	16g
of which saturates	3g
Salt	0.8g
Fibre	6g

Wholemeal cheesy chicken, squash, and chard pasties

These simple, hearty pasties turn leftover chicken into a tasty, portable meal, fantastic for picnics and packed lunches.

INGREDIENTS

For the pastry

125g (4¹/₂oz) wholemeal flour

125g (4¹/₂oz) plain flour, plus extra for dusting

¹/₂ tsp salt

125g (4¹/₂oz) butter, chilled and diced

1 egg, beaten, to glaze

For the filling

1 tbsp olive oil

¹/₂ onion, finely chopped

100g (3¹/₂oz) butternut squash, coarsely grated

1 garlic clove, crushed

2 tbsp plain flour

250ml (9fl oz) skimmed milk

50g (1³/₄oz) strong cheese, grated

100g (3¹/₂oz) Swiss chard, deribbed and finely shredded

250g (9oz) cooked chicken, shredded

SERVES 6    **PREP** 30 MINS, PLUS CHILLING   **COOK** 45–50 MINS

1 For the pastry, sift both lots of flour and the salt into a large mixing bowl. Rub in the butter with your fingertips until the mixture resembles fine breadcrumbs. Make a well in the centre of the mixture and add 3–4 tablespoons of cold water. Bring the mixture together to form a smooth dough, using a little extra water if necessary. Wrap in cling film and chill for 30 minutes.

2 For the filling, heat the oil in a large, non-stick frying pan. Cook the onion over a medium heat for 3 minutes, until softened, but not browned. Add the squash and cook for 2 more minutes, stirring until it starts to soften. Add the garlic and cook for a another minute.

3 Remove from the heat, sprinkle the flour over the vegetables, and mix well. Stir in the milk, a little at a time, until well combined. Cook over a low heat for 2–3 minutes, stirring frequently, until the sauce has thickened. Add the cheese and cook briefly until it melts. Fold the Swiss chard into the sauce, and continue to cook until it has wilted. Remove from the heat, stir in the chicken, season to taste, and set aside to cool. Preheat the oven to 180°C (350°F/Gas 4).

4 On a well-floured surface, cut the pastry into 6 equal pieces. Roll each piece out to a thickness of 5mm (¹/₄in). Using a small plate or saucer (about 15cm/6in in diameter), cut out a circle from each piece of rolled pastry. Place one-sixth of the cooled chicken mixture in the centre of each circle, leaving a 1cm (¹/₂in) border around the edge. Brush the edges with a little beaten egg, bring together to seal, and use your fingers to crimp the edges. Repeat for all pasties.

5 Place the pasties on a non-stick baking sheet, brush the outsides with a little more beaten egg, and cook in the centre of the oven for 35–40 minutes, until golden brown and cooked through.

Nutrition data per serving

Energy	462kcals/1934kJ
Carbohydrate	32g
of which sugar	4g
Fat	28g
of which saturates	15g
Salt	1g
Fibre	4g

Roasted chicken and root vegetables

Roast chicken deserves star treatment, and here a simple
tray of vegetables makes a tasty accompaniment.

INGREDIENTS

1.5kg (3lb 3oz) whole chicken

salt and freshly ground
black pepper

1 small lemon, halved

4 garlic cloves, skin on, crushed
with the side of a knife

1 tbsp olive oil

For the vegetables

8 small new potatoes, halved

4 carrots, cut into 4cm (1½in)
chunks

2 leeks, white part only, cut into
4cm (1½in) chunks

2 parsnips, cut into 4cm (1½in)
chunks

2 small onions, roots intact,
trimmed and cut into
quarters

2 tbsp olive oil

1 tbsp thyme leaves

SERVES 4   **PREP** 15 MINS   **COOK** 1 HR 10 MINS,
PLUS RESTING

1 Preheat the oven to 240°C (475°F/Gas 9). Rinse the chicken, inside
and out, and pat dry with kitchen paper. Season the cavity with
plenty of salt and pepper, and place the lemon and the garlic inside it.
Rub the chicken skin with the oil and season well. Place the chicken in
an oven-proof pan and roast for 25 minutes.

2 Meanwhile, place all the vegetables, oil, and thyme in a large bowl.
Season well and toss until the vegetables are well coated in the oil.

3 Remove the chicken from the oven and reduce the heat to
200°C (400°F/Gas 6). Add the vegetables to the pan and spread
them evenly around the chicken. Roast for a further 45 minutes, until
the vegetables are done, the chicken is golden brown, and the juices run
clear when the thickest part of the thigh is pierced with a metal skewer.

4 Remove the chicken from the pan and leave to rest for 10 minutes
before carving. If the vegetables need further cooking, return them
to the hot oven until cooked. Turn off the heat and keep the vegetables
in the warm oven while the chicken is resting.

Cook's tip: Serve as it is, or with a simple dark green, leafy salad of rocket and
watercress with a citrus dressing.

Nutrition data per serving

Energy	519 kcals/2173kJ
Carbohydrate	37g
of which sugar	16g
Fat	15g
of which saturates	3g
Salt	0.6g
Fibre	11.5g

Mediterranean chicken

This colourful one-pot meal is stuffed full of vitamin-rich vegetables, pleasing the eye as well as the palate.

INGREDIENTS

250g (9oz) butternut squash, peeled and cut into 3cm (1in) cubes

1 red pepper, cut into 3cm (1in) cubes

1 yellow pepper, cut into 3cm (1in) cubes

2 small red onions, quartered

400g (14oz) small new potatoes, halved

2 tbsp olive oil, plus extra for greasing

1 tbsp chopped flat-leaf parsley

salt and freshly ground black pepper

8 skin-on bone-in chicken thighs

1 small punnet of cherry tomatoes, approx. 300g (10oz)

2 tbsp chopped basil leaves

4 small sprigs of rosemary

SERVES 4 **PREP** 20 MINS **COOK** 1 HR

1 Preheat the oven to 180°C (350°F/Gas 4). In a large metal roasting tin, mix the squash, peppers, onions, and potatoes with the olive oil and parsley. Season them well and spread out in a single layer.

2 Rub the chicken thighs with a little oil, season them, and poke into the layer of vegetables.

3 Roast in the oven for 40 minutes. Remove from the oven and increase the oven temperature to 200°C (400°F/Gas 6).

4 Mix in the tomatoes and basil, with a further splash of olive oil if necessary, and tuck in the rosemary. Spread it all out and cook for a further 15–20 minutes at the top of the oven, until the chicken is crisp and the tomatoes are just starting to burst. Remove the rosemary and serve.

Nutrition data per serving

Energy	428kcals/1795kJ
Carbohydrate	29g
of which sugar	12.5g
Fat	18g
of which saturates	4g
Salt	0.4g
Fibre	6g

Creamy mushroom chicken

A deliciously quick supper, perfect served with fluffy mashed
potatoes to soak up all the tasty juices.

INGREDIENTS

3 tbsp olive oil

1 tbsp butter

200g (7oz) button mushrooms,
    sliced

1 onion, finely chopped

2 garlic cloves, finely chopped

1 heaped tbsp plain flour

salt and freshly ground black
    pepper

600g (1lb 5oz) skinless boneless
    chicken thighs, cut into
    3cm (1in) pieces

100ml (3½fl oz) white wine
    (optional)

200ml (7fl oz) chicken stock

1 tbsp finely chopped sage leaves

3 tbsp double cream

SERVES 4    **PREP** 20-25 MINS   **COOK** 15 MINS

1 Heat 1 tbsp of the olive oil and the butter in a large, deep-sided
frying pan. Fry the mushrooms for 5 minutes until they start to
brown. Add the onion and cook for 2–3 minutes until it softens. Add
the garlic, cook for 1 minute, then remove the vegetables from the pan.
Wipe the pan clean with kitchen paper.

2 Heat the remaining 2 tbsp of oil in the pan. Season the flour with
salt and pepper. Toss the chicken in the flour, shaking off excess.
Fry the chicken for 8–10 minutes, turning, until golden all over. Add
the wine (if using), stock, and sage and bubble up.

3 Add the mushroom mixture and simmer for 5 minutes, stirring
occasionally, until the sauce starts to reduce. Add the cream and
cook for 2–3 minutes until the chicken is cooked and the sauce is
thick and creamy.

Nutrition data per serving	
Energy	377kcals/1572kJ
Carbohydrate	5g
of which sugar	1.8g
Fat	22g
of which saturates	8g
Salt	0.6g
Fibre	1.5g

American meatloaf

A sterling family meal. Any leftovers can be fried in
a little oil for a quick supper the following day.

INGREDIENTS

1 onion

1 celery stick

1 carrot

2 tbsp olive oil, plus extra
for greasing

1 garlic clove, crushed

50g (1¾oz) fresh
white breadcrumbs

300g (10oz) minced beef

300g (10oz) minced pork

2 tbsp finely chopped parsley

½ tsp dried thyme, or 1 tbsp
chopped thyme leaves

1 tsp Worcestershire sauce

2 tbsp tomato ketchup

salt and freshly ground
black pepper

SERVES 4 **PREP** 20 MINS **COOK** 1 HR

1 Preheat the oven to 180°C (350°F/Gas 4). If you have a food
processor, roughly chop the onion, celery, and carrot, then process
until very finely chopped. If not, chop as finely as you can.

2 Heat the oil in a saucepan and fry the chopped vegetables over a
low heat for 5 minutes, until they darken slightly. Add the garlic
and cook for 1 minute.

3 Next, mix the vegetables, breadcrumbs, and remaining ingredients
until well mixed, but not compacted.

4 Either line a shallow-sided baking tray with greaseproof paper and
shape the meat into an oval loaf with your hands, or lightly pack it
into an oiled 900g (2lb) loaf tin. Rub oil on top and bake in the middle of
the oven for 45 minutes (1 hour if in a tin). Rest for 10 minutes, then slice
with a sharp, serrated knife and serve with tomato sauce or creamy gravy.

Nutrition data per serving	
Energy	429kcals/1788kJ
Carbohydrate	13g
of which sugar	4g
Fat	28g
of which saturates	9g
Salt	0.8g
Fibre	1g

Sausage and tomato tart

Skinned sausages make the basis of the filling for this delicious tart, guaranteed to please all the family.

INGREDIENTS

225g (8oz) ready-made
    shortcrust pastry
plain flour, for dusting
1 egg, lightly beaten
½ tbsp olive oil
1 onion, finely chopped
400g (14oz) good-quality
    pork sausages, skinned
salt and freshly ground
    black pepper
1 tsp dried oregano
4 tomatoes, sliced

SERVES 4    **PREP** 15 MINS    **COOK** 40 MINS,
                                                       PLUS COOLING

1 Preheat the oven to 200°C (400°F/Gas 6). Roll out the pastry on a floured work surface, and use to line a 20cm (8in) square pie dish. Trim away excess, line the pastry shell with greaseproof paper, and fill with baking beans. Bake in the oven for 15–20 minutes until the edges are golden. Remove the beans and paper, brush the pastry with a little beaten egg, and return to the oven for 2 minutes to crisp. Set aside. Reduce the oven temperature to 180°C (350°F/Gas 4).

2 Meanwhile, heat the oil in a large frying pan over a low heat. Add the onion and cook gently for about 5 minutes until soft. Add the sausage, breaking it up with a fork or the back of a spatula. Season well, and add the oregano. Cook, stirring, over a medium-low heat for 10 minutes, until brown. Leave to cool, then mix in the remaining egg.

3 Spoon the sausage mixture into the pastry shell, then layer the tomatoes over the top. Bake in the oven for about 20 minutes until lightly golden. Leave to cool for 10 minutes before slicing.

Nutrition data per serving

Energy	557kcals/2323kJ
Carbohydrate	35g
of which sugar	6g
Fat	38g
of which saturates	13g
Salt	2.5g
Fibre	3g

Cinnamon and ginger beef with noodles

A quick dish with punchy flavours.

INGREDIENTS

500g (1lb 2oz) lean steak, thinly sliced

2 tsp ground cinnamon

1 tbsp sunflower oil

1 onion, sliced

5cm (2in) piece of fresh ginger, peeled and shredded

1 red chilli, deseeded and finely chopped

2 garlic cloves, finely chopped

1 tbsp fish sauce

1 tbsp sesame oil

200g (7oz) mixed exotic mushrooms, such as oyster, shiitake and hon shimeji, trimmed or chopped

200g mange tout

400g (14oz) medium or thick straight-to-wok udon noodles

SERVES 4 **PREP** 10 MINS **COOK** 15 MINS

1 Put the steak in a bowl, sprinkle over the cinnamon and stir to coat. Heat the sunflower oil in a wok, add the onion, and stir-fry over a high heat for 1 minute. Add the ginger and chilli and stir-fry for a further minute.

2 Now add the steak, garlic, fish sauce, and sesame oil and continue to cook, stirring, until the meat is no longer pink. Add the mushrooms and mange tout and continue to stir-fry for a further 1–2 minutes.

3 Add the noodles and stir-fry for about 3 minutes until the noodles become sticky. Serve immediately.

Cook's tip: Always cook quickly over a high heat when using a wok, and have all your ingredients to hand.

Nutrition data per serving	
Energy	378kcals/1584kJ
Carbohydrate	33g
of which sugar	2.5g
Fat	12g
of which saturates	3g
Salt	1.2g
Fibre	2.2g

Pork tenderloin with apple gravy

An updated version of an old dinner party classic, this family-friendly version uses apple juice instead of wine.

INGREDIENTS

2 tbsp plain flour

salt and freshly ground black
    pepper

450g (1lb) piece of pork tenderloin,
    sliced into 2cm (¾in) pieces

1 tbsp olive oil

2 tbsp butter

150ml (5fl oz) apple juice

150ml (5fl oz) chicken stock

4 tbsp single cream

1 tbsp finely chopped
    sage leaves

SERVES 4    **PREP** 5 MINS   **COOK** 5 MINS

1 Season 1 tbsp of the flour with salt and pepper and place on a plate. Toss the meat in it, lightly coating all sides, and shaking off any excess flour. Preheat the oven to 130°C (250°F/Gas ½).

2 Heat the olive oil and 1 tbsp of the butter in a large, deep-sided frying pan. Sear the pork pieces a few at a time for 2–3 minutes on each side until well browned. You will need to work in batches, as the pan must not be crowded or the meat will fail to form a good crust. Keep the cooked pork warm, loosely covered with foil, in the low oven.

3 Heat the remaining 1 tbsp of butter in the pan and whisk in the remaining 1 tbsp of flour. Whisk in the apple juice and stock, a little at a time, and bring to the boil. Reduce the heat to a simmer and reduce the sauce to about half its original volume, then add the cream and sage, and cook until the sauce is thick and creamy. Season to taste.

4 Return the meat to the pan with any juices that have come from it, and cook for a further minute or 2 until the pork is piping hot once more, and the sauce is evenly glossy. Sautéed potatoes and green beans make good accompaniments.

Nutrition data per serving	
Energy	296kcals/1239kJ
Carbohydrate	9g
of which sugar	4g
Fat	16g
of which saturates	8g
Salt	0.4g
Fibre	0.5g

Pork chops with salsa verde

A simple recipe for juicy pork.

INGREDIENTS

large handful of flat-leaf parsley
handful of fresh basil leaves
handful of fresh mint leaves
2 tbsp red wine vinegar
2 garlic cloves, roughly chopped
2 anchovy fillets
2 tbsp capers, drained and rinsed
3–4 tbsp olive oil
4 lean pork chops, trimmed of fat
salt and freshly ground
    black pepper

SERVES 4 **PREP** 10 MINS **COOK** 10-12 MINS

1 Add the herbs, vinegar, garlic, anchovies, capers, and most of the olive oil to a food processor and whiz until chopped. Spoon out and transfer to a dish.

2 Rub the pork chops with a splash of the remaining oil and season well with salt and black pepper. Heat a griddle pan until hot, add the chops and leave undisturbed for 3–5 minutes, depending on their thickness, then turn them and cook the other side for the same length of time again or until they are no longer pink and are cooked through.

3 Serve the chops topped with the salsa verde and with a mixed salad on the side.

Nutrition data per serving

Energy	266kcals/1115kJ
Carbohydrate	0.5g
of which sugar	0g
Fat	15g
of which saturates	3g
Salt	1.1g
Fibre	0g

Turkey and white bean chilli

This tasty and nourishing version of a traditional chilli is fantastic served over rice, with a shredded salad.

INGREDIENTS

200g (7oz) dried haricot beans

4 tbsp olive oil

1 onion, finely chopped

1 celery stick, trimmed
and finely chopped

1 large leek, trimmed and
finely chopped

2 garlic cloves, finely chopped

1–2 mild green chillies, deseeded
and finely chopped

450g (1lb) minced turkey

1 tbsp plain flour

2 tsp ground cumin

1 tsp ground coriander

½ tsp dried oregano

½ tsp cayenne pepper

750ml (1lb 10oz) chicken stock

2 tbsp finely chopped
flat-leaf parsley

juice of 1 lime, plus 1 lime quartered,
to serve

3 tbsp coriander, finely chopped

4 spring onions, trimmed and
finely chopped

soured cream, to serve

SERVES 4   **PREP 20 MINS, PLUS SOAKING**   **COOK 1 HR**

1 Place the dried beans in a large bowl, cover them well with cold water, and leave to soak overnight. Drain and rinse the beans. Place them in a small, heavy-based saucepan and cover them with water to a depth of at least 3cm (1¼in). Bring them to the boil and cook for 15 minutes, until they are partially softened. Skim the surface of any residue, drain and rinse the beans, and set aside.

2 Meanwhile, to make the chilli, heat 2 tablespoons of the oil in a large, heavy-based saucepan. Cook the onion and celery over a medium heat for 5 minutes, until softened, but not brown. Add the leeks, garlic, and green chillies and cook for 1 minute. Add the remaining oil and the minced turkey. Use a wooden spoon to break up the meat and move it around the pan, until well browned.

3 Stir in the flour, cumin, coriander, oregano, and cayenne pepper to the meat, and cook for 1–2 minutes to allow the spices to release their flavour. Add the stock, partially cooked beans, and parsley to the pan and bring to the boil, stirring well to release any residue at the bottom of the pan. Reduce to a low simmer and cook, uncovered, for 40–45 minutes, until the beans are soft and the sauce has thickened.

4 Remove from the heat and stir in the lime juice. Stir through most of the coriander and spring onions, reserving a little of each to sprinkle on top. Serve with soured cream, extra lime wedges, and hot sauce on the side.

Cook's tip: Minced chicken can also be used in place of turkey, if you prefer.

Nutrition data per serving

Energy	437kcals/1830kJ
Carbohydrate	30g
of which sugar	4.5g
Fat	13g
of which saturates	2g
Salt	0.8g
Fibre	13g

Oven-baked dal pilaf

This wonderful pilaf takes a little time to prepare, but once it is in the oven it takes care of itself.

INGREDIENTS

100g (3½oz) yellow split peas
salt and freshly ground
    black pepper
200g (7oz) white basmati rice
2 tbsp sunflower oil
2 tbsp butter
1 onion, finely chopped
2 garlic cloves, finely chopped
3cm (1in) piece of fresh root ginger,
    finely chopped
1 red chilli, deseeded and chopped
1 tsp chilli powder
1 tsp ground coriander
1 tsp ground cumin
1 tsp turmeric
4 tbsp plain yogurt
350ml (12fl oz) vegetable stock

SERVES 4   **PREP** 30 MINS   **COOK** 30 MINS

1 Put the split peas in a large pan of boiling salted water and cook, uncovered, for about 20 minutes, or until they are just cooked through. Drain, rinse under cold water, and set aside.

2 Meanwhile, put the rice in a sieve and run it under a cold tap for a couple of minutes, rubbing it together with your fingers, to get rid of excess starch. Drain and set aside.

3 Preheat the oven to 160°C (325°F/Gas 3). Heat the oil and butter in a large flameproof casserole. Fry the onion over a medium heat for 5 minutes, until softened, but not browned. Add the garlic, ginger, and chilli and cook for a further minute. Add the ground spices and cook over a low heat for a minute until they start to smell fragrant. Add the yogurt and cook over a low heat until it reduces and thickens.

4 Add the rice, split peas, and stock, and stir well. Cook in the centre of the hot oven for 30 minutes, stirring halfway, until the rice is cooked and the liquid evaporated. Season to taste, and serve.

Nutrition data per serving	
Energy	392kcals/1638kJ
Carbohydrate	54g
of which sugar	3g
Fat	13g
of which saturates	5g
Salt	0.2g
Fibre	3g

Nasi goreng

If your family likes spicy dishes, try this Indonesian rice recipe. Add extra vegetables if you like.

INGREDIENTS

2 tbsp olive oil

2 eggs

salt and freshly ground
  black pepper

1 red pepper, finely sliced

1 orange pepper, finely sliced

1 garlic clove, finely chopped

4cm (1½in) piece of fresh
  root ginger, finely chopped

1 red chilli, deseeded and
  finely chopped

8 spring onions, finely chopped

150g (5½oz) raw king prawns,
  shelled and deveined

600g (1lb 5oz) cooked white rice

200g (7oz) cooked chicken,
  finely chopped

2 tbsp soy sauce, plus extra
  to serve

SERVES 4    **PREP** 15 MINS   **COOK** 20 MINS

1 Heat 1 tbsp of the oil in a large, non-stick frying pan over a medium heat. Crack the eggs into a small jug, season well, and whisk with a fork.

2 Pour the beaten egg into the pan and swirl it to make a thin omelette. Cook for 3 minutes or until set. Transfer to a plate, cut into ribbons, and set aside.

3 Heat the remaining oil in the pan and add the peppers, garlic, ginger, chilli, and spring onions. Cook over a medium heat for 5 minutes, stirring occasionally.

4 Add the prawns to the pan and stir-fry for 2 minutes. Add the rice, chicken, and soy sauce to the pan and heat for 5 minutes, stirring occasionally, then stir in the omelette ribbons.

5 Serve the nasi goreng in warmed bowls, with extra soy sauce to season.

Nutrition data per serving	
Energy	458kcals/1929kJ
Carbohydrate	49g
of which sugar	5g
Fat	17g
of which saturates	4g
Salt	1.8g
Fibre	2.2g

Spaghetti and meatballs

Spaghetti and meatballs are a family favourite. Covered in a rich tomato sauce, the lean red meat is a great source of iron, while the wholewheat pasta provides extra fibre.

INGREDIENTS

For the meatballs

450g (1lb) lean minced beef

1 small onion, finely chopped

1 garlic clove, crushed

50g (1³⁄₄oz) fresh
white breadcrumbs

25g (scant 1oz) grated
Parmesan cheese

1 tbsp finely chopped thyme

1 tbsp finely chopped oregano

2 tbsp finely chopped
flat-leaf parsley

1 egg, beaten

salt and freshly ground
black pepper

2 tbsp olive oil

For the sauce

1 onion, finely chopped

2 garlic cloves, crushed

2 x 400g can tomatoes, chopped
or crushed

250ml (9fl oz) chicken or beef stock

2 tbsp finely chopped
flat-leaf parsley

300g (10oz) wholewheat spaghetti

SERVES 4  **PREP** 30 MINS, PLUS RESTING **COOK** 1 HR

1 For the meatballs, place all the ingredients in a large bowl, season well, and mix thoroughly with your fingertips. Form 24 walnut-sized meatballs, cover with cling film, and allow to rest for 30 minutes. This will help them retain their shape on cooking. Heat the oil in a large frying pan with high sides. Fry the meatballs over a medium-high heat for 2–3 minutes on each side until they are browned, but not cooked through. Remove them from the heat and set aside.

2 To prepare the sauce, add the onion to the same pan and cook over a low heat for 5 minutes, until softened but not brown. Scrape up any residue left in the pan from the meatballs, as this will flavour the sauce. Add the garlic and cook for 1–2 minutes. Add the tomatoes, stock, and chopped parsley and season well. Bring the sauce to the boil, reduce the heat to a low simmer, and cook for 30 minutes until reduced and thickened. If the sauce looks too thick, add a little water. You can also make the sauce smoother, if you prefer, by either mashing it with a potato masher or using a hand-held blender.

3 Boil a large pan of salted water for the spaghetti and cook according to packet instructions. Add the meatballs to the sauce 10 minutes before the end of the cooking time. Turn them so that they are well covered in the sauce, reduce the heat to a low simmer, and cook, covered, until the spaghetti is ready. Drain the spaghetti and toss with the meatballs and sauce before serving with extra Parmesan, if you like.

Cook's tip: It is easy to make double the meatballs, then open freeze half of them on a tray. Once frozen, pack them into freezer bags for later use.

Nutrition data per serving

Energy	510kcals/2135kJ
Carbohydrate	60g
of which sugar	8g
Fat	15g
of which saturates	5g
Salt	0.9g
Fibre	10.5g

Conchigliette with sausage and tomato sauce

Sausages are an easy standby, but can get boring. Skin them and mix into this child-friendly, easy pasta sauce.

INGREDIENTS

1 tbsp olive oil
1 red onion, finely chopped
2 garlic cloves, finely chopped
8 pork and herb sausages, skinned
1 tsp dried oregano
1 tsp dried marjoram
½ tsp fennel seeds
salt and freshly ground
   black pepper
2 x 500g cartons passata
150g (5½oz) dried conchigliette
   or other small pasta shapes
finely grated Parmesan cheese,
   garlic bread, and salad, to serve

SERVES 4    **PREP** 10 MINS    **COOK** 30-40 MINS

1 Heat the oil in a large pan over a medium heat and fry the onion for 5 minutes, until translucent and softened, but not browned.

2 Add the garlic, sausages, oregano, marjoram, and fennel seeds. Season and stir well, breaking the sausages up with a wooden spoon so the meat browns all over. Cook over a medium heat for 5 minutes, stirring constantly so it does not catch. Add the passata, cover, and simmer for 10 minutes.

3 Add the conchigliette and cook over a low heat for 10 minutes, or until cooked, stirring regularly. If the mixture threatens to become too dry, add a splash of water.

4 Spoon into bowls, sprinkle generously with Parmesan cheese, and serve with garlic bread, and a green salad.

Nutrition data per serving

Energy	510kcals/2136kJ
Carbohydrate	48g
of which sugar	4g
Fat	25g
of which saturates	8.5g
Salt	2.1g
Fibre	5g

Smoked salmon and crème fraîche pasta

A simple yet stylish way to pull together a fabulous supper
with just a few ingredients from the fridge.

INGREDIENTS

300g (10oz) dried pasta
salt and freshly ground
    black pepper
200ml (7fl oz) half-fat crème fraîche
120g (4oz) smoked salmon,
    finely chopped
1 tbsp finely chopped capers,
    rinsed, or more to taste
finely grated zest of ½ lemon
2 tbsp finely chopped dill
finely grated Parmesan cheese,
    to serve

SERVES 4   **PREP** 5 MINS   **COOK** 10 MINS

1 Cook the pasta in a large pan of boiling salted water according to the packet instructions.

2 Meanwhile, beat the crème fraîche in a bowl until smooth. Add the smoked salmon, capers, lemon zest, and dill, and season.

3 Drain the pasta (reserving a ladleful of the cooking water) and return it to the pan with the reserved water. Toss the sauce through the pasta and return it to the heat, stirring just long enough for the pasta to soak up some of the sauce and for the sauce to heat through. Serve with the Parmesan cheese.

Nutrition data per serving

Energy	2510kcals/2142kJ
Carbohydrate	54g
of which sugar	3g
Fat	25g
of which saturates	15g
Salt	1.2g
Fibre	2.2g

Tomato and mascarpone pasta

This is a perfect way to use up over-ripe tomatoes.

INGREDIENTS

salt and freshly ground black
  pepper
300g (10oz) dried pasta
4 large, over-ripe tomatoes, approx.
  600g (1lb 5oz) in total, skinned
  and cubed
2 tbsp olive oil
2 garlic cloves, crushed
4 heaped tbsp mascarpone
4 tbsp finely grated Parmesan
  cheese
2 tbsp roughly chopped
  basil leaves

SERVES 4  **PREP** 10 MINS  **COOK** 10-15 MINS

1 Bring a large pan of salted water to the boil and cook the pasta according to the packet instructions.

2 Heat the oil in a large frying pan. Add the tomatoes and garlic and fry for 2 minutes until they start to break down.

3 Add 200ml (7fl oz) of water and cook over a high heat for about 5 minutes, or until the tomatoes have completely broken down and the sauce is very thick. Drain the pasta and return it to the pan.

4 Season the sauce well and stir in the mascarpone. Cook for a further minute or two until the mascarpone has dispersed and the sauce is thick and creamy. Toss through the pasta and cook over a low heat for 2 minutes until the pasta has absorbed some of the sauce. Take it off the heat, toss through the Parmesan cheese and basil, and serve.

Nutrition data per serving

Energy	460kcals/1942kJ
Carbohydrate	58g
of which sugar	7g
Fat	18g
of which saturates	8g
Salt	0.4g
Fibre	5g

Roasted butternut squash and mushroom lasagne

This colourful winter warmer is a healthy twist on a family favourite. For a richer, earthy flavour, try wholemeal lasagne sheets and a mild blue cheese.

INGREDIENTS

600g (1lb 5oz) butternut squash, peeled and cut into 1.5cm (½in) cubes

400g (14oz) chestnut mushrooms, halved or quartered

2 red onions, roughly chopped

4 tbsp olive oil

2 tbsp finely chopped sage

salt and freshly ground black pepper

For the sauce

50g (1¾oz) butter

50g (1¾oz) plain flour

450ml (14fl oz) skimmed milk

75g (2½oz) grated strong cheese, such as Cheddar

100g (3½oz) (about 6 sheets) precooked lasagne

SERVES 4-6    **PREP 20-25 MINS**   **COOK 1 HR 15 MINS**

1 Preheat the oven to 200°C (400°F/Gas 6). Mix the squash, mushrooms, and red onions in the oil, and toss together with the sage, salt, and pepper. Spread the vegetables out in a large roasting pan, and roast them at the top of the oven for 30 minutes, turning them once, until soft. Remove from the oven and set aside to cool.

2 For the sauce, melt the butter in a small, heavy-based saucepan. Remove from the heat and whisk in the flour. Whisk in the milk, a little at a time, until the sauce is smooth. Return the pan to the heat and cook, stirring constantly, until the sauce has thickened. Reduce the heat to low and continue to cook, stirring occasionally, for 5 minutes. Add two-thirds of the grated cheese, season well, and cook for a further 2–3 minutes until thick and creamy.

3 Reduce the temperature to 180°C (350°F/Gas 4). To construct the lasagne, spread one-third of the sauce at the bottom of a 20cm (8in) square ovenproof dish. Cover with half the vegetables, then a layer of lasagne. Repeat the process, finishing with a layer of sauce on top. Sprinkle the remaining cheese over the top and bake in the oven for 45 minutes to 1 hour, until it is well browned on top and soft when pierced with a knife. Remove from the oven and allow it to rest for 5 minutes before serving.

Cook's tip: Lasagne can be time-consuming to make. Get ahead by roasting the vegetables (step 1) up to a day before, and store them in the fridge in an airtight container until needed.

Nutrition data per serving

Energy	519 kcals/2173 kJ
Carbohydrate	48g
of which sugar	15g
Fat	29g
of which saturates	12g
Salt	0.7g
Fibre	7g

Brown rice, red pepper, and artichoke risotto

Not a risotto in the true sense, but a great mix of flavours and textures.

INGREDIENTS

1 tbsp olive oil

1 onion, finely chopped

salt and freshly ground black pepper

2 sweet pointed red peppers, halved, deseeded and chopped

pinch of chilli flakes

280g (10oz) brown rice

1 litre (1¾ pints) vegetable stock

280g jar of artichoke hearts, drained and roughly chopped

handful of flat-leaf parsley, finely chopped

SERVES 4  **PREP** 10 MINS  **COOK** 50 MINS–1 HR

1 Heat the oil in a large frying pan then add the onion and cook on a low heat until soft and transparent. Season with a pinch of salt and some freshly ground black pepper. Add the red peppers and cook for a few minutes until they soften.

2 Add the chilli flakes, then stir in the rice. Raise the heat a little, pour in a ladleful of the stock, and bring to the boil. Reduce to a simmer and cook gently for 40–50 minutes, adding a little more stock each time the liquid is absorbed, until the rice is cooked.

3 Stir through the artichokes and cook for a couple of minutes to heat through, then taste and season as required. Cover with a lid, remove from the heat and leave for 10 minutes, then stir through the chopped parsley and transfer to plates or bowls. You could serve this with a rocket salad on the side.

Cook's tip: Artichokes bought in a jar will taste far better than the canned ones. Do save the oil as you can use it for a dressing. If you can't find the pointed peppers, use regular peppers – they're just as tasty but not quite as sweet.

Nutrition data per serving

Energy	406kcals/1713kJ
Carbohydrate	67g
of which sugar	9g
Fat	13.5g
of which saturates	1g
Salt	1.2g
Fibre	4g

Mushroom, leek, and red pepper filo pie

A layered pie to be eaten hot or cold.

INGREDIENTS

1 tbsp oil, plus extra for brushing
1 onion, finely chopped
salt and freshly ground
   black pepper
small handful fresh thyme,
   finely chopped
1 leek, finely sliced
2 red peppers, finely chopped
250g (9oz) mushrooms
   (chestnut and oyster varieties;
   keep them separate), chopped
150ml (5fl oz) vegetable stock
about 18 sheets filo pastry
butter, melted, for brushing

MAKES 4    **PREP** 15 MINS   **COOK** 40 MINS

1 Preheat the oven to 190°C (375°F/Gas 5). Heat the oil in a large frying pan then add the onion, season with salt and black pepper, and add the thyme. Cook over a low heat for 2–3 minutes until the onion begins to soften, then stir in the leek and red peppers and cook for 5–8 minutes more.

2 Add the chestnut mushrooms and cook for 5 minutes or until they begin to release their juices, then add the oyster mushrooms and cook for 2 minutes more. Pour in a little stock, increase the heat and allow to bubble, then gradually add the rest and cook until the liquid is almost soaked up.

3 Lay a double layer of filo pastry sheets in a small-to-medium oblong pie dish or roasting tin to cover the base (about 6 sheets), and brush with oil. Spoon over half the mixture, then arrange another double layer of pastry sheets on top and brush with oil. Repeat with the remaining mixture and a third double layer of pastry, tucking the edges down the sides of the dish. Brush liberally with melted butter and transfer to the oven to cook for 20–25 minutes until golden and crispy. Cut into 4 portions and serve. You might try it with a dressed mixed salad on the side.

Cook's tip: This brittle pastry requires oiling so it doesn't break up. If you prefer not to oil, work quickly between layering and keep the filo wrapped in cling film.

Nutrition data per serving

Energy	259kcals/1078kJ
Carbohydrate	35g
of which sugar	10g
Fat	10g
of which saturates	2.5g
Salt	0.7g
Fibre	3g

Butternut squash and spinach curry

A mildly spiced, low-fat curry, rich in B vitamins and betacarotene,
which the body can convert to Vitamin A.

INGREDIENTS

2 tbsp vegetable oil

1 large onion, peeled and chopped

1 medium butternut squash, about
   1.25kg (2³/₄lb), peeled and cut
   into 2cm (³/₄in) cubes

2 cloves garlic, peeled and crushed

2–3 tbsp curry paste

400g can chopped tomatoes

360ml (12fl oz) vegetable stock
   or chicken stock

225g (8oz) bag fresh washed
   baby spinach

salt and freshly ground
   black pepper

SERVES 6   **PREP** 15 MINS   **COOK** 30-35 MINS

1 Heat the oil in a large, deep pan, add the onion and cook gently for
2–3 minutes. Add the butternut squash, garlic, and curry paste and
cook for a further 2–3 minutes.

2 Add the tomatoes and stock. Bring to the boil, then reduce the heat,
cover, and simmer for 15 minutes, stirring occasionally. Remove
the lid and simmer for a further 10 minutes. Add a little extra stock or
water if it becomes too dry.

3 Stir in the spinach, cover and cook for 1–2 minutes until just wilted.
Season to taste with salt and pepper and spoon into serving bowls.
If desired, you could add a spoonful of yogurt to serve.

Nutrition data per serving

Energy	194kcals/817kJ
Carbohydrate	26g
of which sugar	16g
Fat	8g
of which saturates	0.8g
Salt	0.6g
Fibre	6g

Vegetable moussaka

Lentils replace the lamb, and yogurt is a light alternative
to béchamel sauce, in this vegetarian version.

INGREDIENTS

2 aubergines, about 600g (1lb 5oz)
   in total, cut into 1cm (½in) slices

2 courgettes, thickly sliced

2 onions, thickly sliced

2 red peppers, cored, deseeded,
   and thickly sliced

4 tbsp olive oil

salt and freshly ground
   black pepper

2 garlic cloves, coarsely chopped

1 tbsp chopped thyme leaves

400g can chopped tomatoes

300g can green lentils, drained
   and rinsed

2 tbsp chopped flat-leaf parsley

2 eggs, lightly beaten

300g (10oz) Greek-style yogurt

pinch of paprika

85g (3oz) feta cheese, crumbled

2 tbsp white sesame seeds

SERVES 4  **PREP** 20 MINS  **COOK** 1 HR 30 MINS

1 Preheat the oven to 220°C (425°F/Gas 7). Place the aubergines, courgettes, onions, and red peppers into a roasting tin. Drizzle over the olive oil, toss together to coat the vegetables evenly, then season to taste with salt and pepper.

2 Roast for 10 minutes, toss, add the garlic and thyme, and roast for a further 30–35 minutes, or until the vegetables are tender. Reduce the temperature to 180°C (350°F/Gas 4).

3 Stir the tomatoes with their juices, the lentils, and the parsley into the roast vegetables. Taste and adjust the seasoning, if necessary. Transfer the vegetables to a 23cm (9in) square ovenproof serving dish.

4 Beat the eggs and yogurt with the paprika, and season to taste with salt and pepper. Spread the mixture over the vegetables, and sprinkle the feta cheese on top. Put the dish on a baking tray and bake for 40 minutes. Sprinkle with the sesame seeds and bake for 10 minutes, or until the top is golden. Leave to stand for at least 2 minutes, then serve while still warm.

Nutrition data per serving	
Energy	505kcals/2103kJ
Carbohydrate	33g
of which sugar	17g
Fat	32g
of which saturates	11.5g
Salt	1.1g
Fibre	8g

Baked gnocchi with cheese sauce

Gnocchi is an excellent standby for any busy family's fridge.
A few additions turn it into something special.

INGREDIENTS

40g (1¼oz) butter
40g (1¼oz) plain flour
500ml (16fl oz) whole milk
1 tsp English mustard
70g (2¼oz) grated
    Gruyère cheese
salt and freshly ground
    black pepper
500g (1lb 2oz)
    shop-bought gnocchi
150g (5½oz) bocconcini (small
    mozzarella cheese balls)
100g (3½oz) cherry
    tomatoes, halved
green salad, to serve

SERVES 4  **PREP 10 MINS**  **COOK 25 MINS**

1 Preheat the oven to 200°C (400°F/Gas 6). Melt the butter in a pan. Whisk in the flour over a low heat. Cook for 2 minutes, whisking constantly, until the mixture bubbles and separates.

2 Take the pan off the heat and whisk in the milk, a little at a time, whisking well between each addition, until it has all been added and the sauce is smooth. Return to the heat and cook, stirring constantly, until it thickens. Reduce the heat to low and cook, stirring occasionally, for 5 minutes. Be sure to whisk right into the edges of the saucepan, as this is where the sauce can burn if left undisturbed.

3 Add the mustard and Gruyère cheese and stir until the cheese has melted and the sauce is smooth, thick, and creamy. Season well.

4 Place the gnocchi in a shallow ovenproof dish, pour over the sauce, and arrange the mozzarella balls and cherry tomatoes, cut-side up, on top. Bake for 15 minutes. Spoon onto warmed plates and serve with a green salad.

Nutrition data per serving	
Energy	555kcals/2314kJ
Carbohydrate	53g
of which sugar	7g
Fat	27g
of which saturates	17g
Salt	2.4g
Fibre	3g

Root vegetable crumble

This creamy, homely dish is an easy and deliciously satisfying
way to increase the amount of autumnal and winter
vegetables in your family's diet.

SERVES 4    **PREP** 30 MINS   **COOK** 50 MINS

INGREDIENTS

1kg (2¼lb) mixed root
    vegetables, such as carrots,
    potatoes, turnips, parsnips,
    celeriac, sweet potatoes,
    swede, and squash, cut into
    1.5cm (¾in) chunks

50g (1¾oz) butter

50g (1¾oz) plain flour

450ml (15fl oz) skimmed milk

100g (3½oz) grated
    strong cheese

1 tsp Dijon mustard,
    or more to taste

1 tsp grain mustard, or
    more to taste

salt and freshly ground
    black pepper

50g (1¾oz) fresh white or
    wholemeal bread, torn
    into rough chunks

25g (scant 1oz) rolled oats

25g (scant 1oz) grated
    Parmesan cheese

1 tbsp olive oil

1 Preheat the oven to 180°C (350°F/Gas 4). Cook the vegetables in a
large pan of boiling, salted water for 10 minutes, until partially
cooked. Drain them well and return to the pan.

2 Meanwhile, make the sauce. Melt the butter in a small, heavy-based
saucepan. Reduce the heat to low and whisk in the flour. Cook the
mixture over a low heat, whisking constantly, until it bubbles and
separates under the whisk.

3 Remove the pan from the heat and slowly whisk in the milk, a little
at a time, until it is incorporated and smooth. Return the pan to the
heat and cook the sauce over a medium heat, stirring constantly, until
it thickens. Reduce the heat to low and continue to cook, stirring
occasionally, for 3–5 minutes. Add the cheese and both mustards, and
season well. Cook for a further 1–2 minutes, until the cheese has melted.

4 Pour the sauce over the cooked vegetables, and gently turn them
so they are well coated. Pile the vegetables into a 20cm x 25cm
(8in x 10in) ovenproof dish (or similar) and smooth the top down.

5 For the topping, place the bread chunks, oats, and Parmesan
in a food processor and season well. Process until the mixture
resembles rough breadcrumbs. Tip the mixture onto the vegetables
and smooth them over. Drizzle with the olive oil and bake in the oven
for 35–40 minutes, until the top is golden brown and crispy and the
vegetables are bubbling.

Nutrition data per serving

Energy	467kcals/1955kJ
Carbohydrate	39g
of which sugar	15g
Fat	26g
of which saturates	14g
Salt	1.4g
Fibre	11g

Kasha pilaf

Kasha is a healthy and delicious wholegrain cereal
that is prepared similarly to risotto.

INGREDIENTS

2 tbsp polyunsaturated
    margarine
1 large onion, chopped
2 celery sticks, sliced
1 large egg
200g (7oz) coarse kasha
    (buckwheat groats) or
    whole kasha
1 tsp ground sage
1 tsp ground thyme
115g (4oz) raisins
115g (4oz) walnut pieces,
    coarsely chopped
salt

SERVES 6   **PREP** 5 MINS    **COOK** 25 MINS

1 In a large frying pan, melt the margarine and gently fry the onion
and celery for 3 minutes, or until the vegetables begin to soften.

2 In a small bowl, mix the egg with the kasha, then add the mixture
to the pan. Cook, stirring constantly, for 1 minute, or until the
grains are dry and separated. Add 500ml (16fl oz) water, the sage, and
the thyme to the kasha. Bring to the boil, then reduce the heat, cover,
and simmer for 10–12 minutes.

3 Stir the raisins and walnuts into the kasha. Cook for a further
4–5 minutes, or until the kasha is tender and all the liquid has
been absorbed. Season to taste with salt.

Nutrition data per serving	
Energy	370kcals/1537kJ
Carbohydrate	45g
of which sugar	15g
Fat	19g
of which saturates	2.5g
Salt	0.2g
Fibre	2g

SWEETS AND SNACKS

Tzatziki

Traditionally served in Greece as a starter with a pile of pitta bread, this dip can also be served with lamb dishes.

INGREDIENTS

10cm (4in) piece of cucumber, quartered lengthways and deseeded

200g (7oz) Greek yogurt or thick plain yogurt

1 tbsp finely chopped mint leaves

1 tbsp finely chopped dill

1 small garlic clove, crushed

1 tbsp lemon juice

salt and freshly ground black pepper

SERVES 4   **PREP 10 MINS**

1 Grate the lengths of cucumber into a sieve, pressing them down to remove most of the excess water.

2 Put the grated cucumber in a clean tea towel and squeeze it well to remove the last of the water. Place the squeezed ball of cucumber on a chopping board and chop it up to make it even finer.

3 Mix it together with the remaining ingredients and season to taste. Cover and chill until needed.

Nutrition data per serving	
Energy	49kcals/203kJ
Carbohydrate	3g
of which sugar	3g
Fat	3g
of which saturates	2g
Salt	0.2g
Fibre	0.2g

Baba ghanoush

Try this delicious smoky Middle Eastern dip with toasted pitta,
or just scooped up with fresh bread.

INGREDIENTS

1 large aubergine
2 tbsp olive oil
1 tbsp lemon juice
3 tbsp tahini
1 garlic clove, crushed
1 tsp smoked paprika
salt and freshly ground
   black pepper
crudités, or toasted pitta,
   to serve

SERVES 4  **PREP** 10 MINS **COOK** 30 MINS,
PLUS COOLING

1 Preheat the oven to 230°C (450°F/Gas 8). Prick the aubergine all over with a fork, then rub it with 1 tbsp of the olive oil. Place on a baking tray and bake at the top of the hot oven for 25–30 minutes, turning once, until the skin has completely blackened and the interior is very soft.

2 Remove the aubergine from the oven and leave it to cool. When it is cold, cut it in half and scoop out the flesh into the bowl of a food processor or blender. Add the remaining ingredients and purée the mixture to a rough paste. Taste and adjust the seasoning. Serve with some crudités or toasted pitta.

Nutrition data per serving	
Energy	129kcals/535kJ
Carbohydrate	2g
of which sugar	1.5g
Fat	12.5g
of which saturates	2g
Salt	trace
Fibre	3g

Broad bean purée

Broad beans are a great source of low-fat protein and fibre, as well as B vitamins. Try serving this purée with oatcakes, rye crackers, or toast.

INGREDIENTS

250g (9oz) skinless dried broad beans, soaked overnight

3 onions

6 garlic cloves

bunch of coriander, chopped, plus extra to garnish

bunch of flat-leaf parsley, chopped, plus extra to garnish

2 tbsp chopped mint

1 tsp ground cumin

salt and freshly ground black pepper

1–3 tbsp olive oil

juice of 1 lemon

SERVES 6    **PREP** 20 MINS    **COOK** 1 HR 15 MINS

1 Drain the beans and place in a large pan. Pour in enough cold water to cover. Roughly chop 1 onion and 3 garlic cloves, add to the pan and then bring to the boil. Skim off any scum and lower the heat, then cover and simmer for 1 hour, or until the beans are soft.

2 Drain the beans, reserving the cooking liquid. Place the beans in a blender or food processor with the coriander, parsley, mint, and cumin. Add salt and pepper to taste and then blend to a smooth purée, adding enough of the reserved cooking liquid to ensure that the mixture is not too dry. Transfer to a serving dish and keep warm.

3 Slice the remaining onions. Heat 1 tablespoon of the oil in a frying pan, add the onions, and fry, stirring frequently, over a medium-high heat for 10–15 minutes or until they are dark golden and slightly caramelized. Chop the remaining garlic finely, add it to the pan and stir-fry for a further minute.

4 Spread the fried onions and garlic over the top of the purée and drizzle with the lemon juice and remaining oil.

Nutrition data per serving

Energy	92kcals/385kJ
Carbohydrate	7g
of which sugar	0.2g
Fat	6g
of which saturates	0.8g
Salt	0.2g
Fibre	3g

Artichoke and spring onion dip

A storecupboard recipe that has sophisticated and subtle
flavours, but takes just minutes to make.

INGREDIENTS

400g can of artichoke hearts,
    drained
1 garlic clove, halved
3 spring onions, coarsely chopped
2 tbsp good-quality mayonnaise
salt and freshly ground black
    pepper

SERVES 6 **PREP** 5 MINS

1 Place the artichokes, garlic, spring onions, and mayonnaise in a food
processor or blender and process to form a smooth purée.

2 Season to taste with salt and pepper, then spoon into a serving
bowl, cover, and refrigerate until ready to use.

Nutrition data per serving	
Energy	48kcals/199kJ
Carbohydrate	2.5g
of which sugar	2.5g
Fat	4g
of which saturates	0.5g
Salt	0.2g
Fibre	1g

Cheese straws

A great way of using up any leftover bits of hard cheese
that may be lurking in the fridge.

INGREDIENTS

75g (2¹/₂oz) plain flour, sifted,
plus extra for dusting

pinch of salt

50g (1³/₄oz) butter, softened
and cut into cubes

30g (1oz) finely grated
mature Cheddar or Red
Leicester cheese

1 egg yolk, lightly beaten,
plus 1 egg, lightly beaten,
for brushing

1 tsp Dijon mustard

MAKES 15-20   **PREP** 10 MINS,
PLUS CHILLING

COOK 15 MINS,
PLUS COOLING

1 Place the flour, salt, and butter in a food processor. Pulse-blend until
the mixture resembles crumbs. Mix in the cheese. Whisk the egg
yolk with 1 tbsp of water and the mustard. Mix it into the crumbs.

2 Turn out onto a floured surface and knead briefly. Wrap in cling
film and chill for 1 hour. Preheat the oven to 200°C (400°F/Gas 6).

3 Roll the dough out to a 30 x 15cm (12 x 6in) rectangle. Cut 1cm-
(½in-) wide strips along the shorter side. Brush with a little egg.
Holding the top of each, twist the bottom a few times to form spirals.

4 Place the straws on non-stick baking sheets, pressing down the
ends. Bake at the top of the oven for 15 minutes. Cool on the trays
for 5 minutes, then transfer to a wire rack. These keep in an airtight
container for up to 3 days.

Nutrition data per serving

Energy	45kcals/189kJ
Carbohydrate	3g
of which sugar	0.1g
Fat	3.5g
of which saturates	1.8g
Salt	0.15g
Fibre	0.2g

No-cook vanilla fudge

This is perfect for younger children to make because it involves
no high temperatures and is easy to handle.

INGREDIENTS

50g (1¾oz) unsalted
   butter, softened
3 heaped tbsp condensed milk,
   or 50g (1¾oz) by weight
½ tsp vanilla extract
225g (8oz) icing sugar, plus extra
   for dusting

MAKES 30   **PREP** 15 MINS,
                      PLUS CHILLING

1 In a large bowl, whisk the softened butter until very smooth using
an electric whisk. Add the condensed milk and vanilla extract and
whisk again. Whisk in the icing sugar a little at a time until it has all
combined to form a lumpy dough.

2 Press the mixture together to form a ball, then place it on a work
surface dusted with icing sugar and knead gently to form a
smooth dough.

3 Lightly dust a rolling pin with icing sugar and roll out the fudge
dough to about 2cm (¾in) thick. Use a 3cm (1in) shaped cutter
to cut out the sweets. Dip the cutter in icing sugar between cuts to
prevent sticking. You will need to re-roll the fudge to cut all the pieces.

4 Transfer the fudge pieces to a plate and leave them to harden,
uncovered, in the fridge for at least 3 hours. Store in an airtight
container in the fridge for up to 1 week.

Nutrition data per serving

Energy	47kcals/200kJ
Carbohydrate	8g
of which sugar	8g
Fat	1.5g
of which saturates	1g
Salt	trace
Fibre	0g

Chocolate-dipped strawberries

A simple fruity snack is all the better after being
dipped in rich, dark chocolate.

INGREDIENTS

400g (14oz) strawberries, not
too ripe
100g (3½oz) good-quality dark
chocolate, more than 60 per cent
cocoa solids, broken into pieces

SERVES 8   **PREP 20 MINS**

1 Wash and dry the strawberries well. Try to leave the hulls in,
as this makes the finished fruit easier to pick up.

2 Put the chocolate in a small heatproof bowl and place over a
saucepan of simmering water, making sure the bowl does not
touch the water. Stir frequently and remove it as soon as it melts.

3 Line a large baking sheet with greaseproof paper. Hold each
strawberry by its leaves and dip the end in the chocolate, so half
of the fruit is covered in chocolate. Allow any excess chocolate to drip
off back into the bowl, then place the strawberries on the baking sheet,
making sure they do not touch each other.

4 Put in a cool place to set. These should be served the same day, as
the chocolate will soften if the strawberries are over-ripe, or if they
are kept in the fridge for too long.

Nutrition data per serving	
Energy	77kcals/324kJ
Carbohydrate	10g
of which sugar	10g
Fat	3.5g
of which saturates	2g
Salt	0g
Fibre	1g

Rocky road squares

These chocolatey treats are very rich, so be sure to cut
them into small party-sized pieces.

INGREDIENTS

250g (9oz) good-quality dark
  chocolate (more than 60% cocoa
  solids), broken into pieces
150g (5¹/₂oz) unsalted butter,
  plus extra for the tin
2 tbsp golden syrup
200g (7oz) rich tea biscuits
50g (1³/₄oz) raisins
50g (1³/₄oz) dried cranberries
100g (3¹/₂oz) mini
  marshmallows

MAKES 36   **PREP 15-20 MINS,
PLUS CHILLING**

1 Put the chocolate, butter, and syrup in a large, heatproof bowl and
melt it over a saucepan of simmering water, making sure the bowl
does not touch the water. When it has melted, leave to cool slightly.

2 Put the biscuits into a plastic bag and bash with a rolling pin until
you have small, broken pieces.

3 Mix the biscuits into the chocolate mixture. Next mix in the dried
fruit and marshmallows.

4 Grease an 18cm (7in) square baking tin with butter and line it with
baking parchment. Turn the mixture into the tin and press it down
firmly with the back of a spoon.

5 Cover and refrigerate for 2 hours, before turning it out and cutting
into 36 squares with a sharp knife. In warm weather, store these in
the fridge.

Nutrition data per serving	
Energy	110kcals/460kJ
Carbohydrate	13g
of which sugar	10g
Fat	6g
of which saturates	4g
Salt	0.1g
Fibre	0.3g

Quick banana ice cream

This is the quickest and easiest ice cream you will
ever make and it's super healthy, too!

INGREDIENTS

4 ripe bananas
1 tsp vanilla extract

SERVES 4   **PREP** 5 MINS,
                                        PLUS FREEZING

1 Simply peel the bananas, chop them into 2cm (¾in) chunks, and put
them in a freezer container. Seal, and put in the freezer until frozen.

2 When the bananas are frozen solid, process them in a food
processor with the vanilla extract, until you have a smooth, thick
ice cream. You may need to scrape down the sides a couple of times
during the process.

3 Either eat the softened banana ice cream immediately, or freeze
for a few minutes for it to firm up once more before serving.

Nutrition data per serving	
Energy	119kcals/504kJ
Carbohydrate	27g
of which sugar	25g
Fat	0g
of which saturates	0g
Salt	trace
Fibre	2g

Creamy custard

The secret to any custard is to heat it gently, so
that the eggs do not scramble.

INGREDIENTS

300ml (10fl oz) whole milk
2 large egg yolks
1 tbsp caster sugar
¼ tsp vanilla extract
1 tsp cornflour

SERVES 4   **PREP** 5 MINS   **COOK** 10 MINS

1 Heat the milk until it is hot, but not boiling. In a bowl, whisk together the egg yolks, sugar, vanilla extract, and cornflour.

2 Gradually pour the hot milk into the eggs in a thin stream, whisking it continuously. Return the mixture to the rinsed-out saucepan and heat over a medium flame, whisking constantly, until it starts to bubble.

3 Reduce the heat to a low simmer and cook for a further 5 minutes, until the mixture thickens and coats the back of a wooden spoon.

Nutrition data per serving

Energy	99kcals/414kJ
Carbohydrate	8g
of which sugar	7g
Fat	6g
of which saturates	3g
Salt	trace
Fibre	0g

Pistachio and cranberry oat cookies

Using pistachios and cranberries brings a healthy, chewy
bite to these easy-to-make cookies.

INGREDIENTS

100g (3½oz) unsalted
  butter, softened
200g (7oz) soft light
  brown sugar
1 egg, lightly beaten
1 tsp vanilla extract
1 tbsp runny honey
125g (4½oz) self-raising
  flour, sifted
125g (4½oz) oats
pinch of salt
100g (3½oz) pistachio nuts,
  lightly toasted and
  roughly chopped
100g (3½oz) dried cranberries,
  roughly chopped
a little milk, if needed

MAKES 24    **PREP** 20 MINS    **COOK** 10-15 MINS

1 Preheat the oven to 190°C (375°F/Gas 5). Put the butter and sugar in a bowl, and cream with an electric hand-held whisk until smooth. Add the egg, vanilla extract, and honey, and beat well.

2 Add the flour, oats, and salt, stirring with a wooden spoon to combine. Add the chopped nuts and cranberries, and mix until thoroughly combined. If the mixture is too stiff, add a little milk until it becomes pliable.

3 Take walnut-sized pieces and roll them into balls between your palms. Place on 2 or 3 baking sheets lined with parchment and flatten slightly, spacing them well apart on the tray.

4 Bake for 10–15 minutes until golden brown (you may need to do this in batches). Leave on the tray to cool, then transfer to a wire rack. These will keep in an airtight container for up to 5 days.

Nutrition data per serving

Energy	145kcals/611kJ
Carbohydrate	19g
of which sugar	12g
Fat	6g
of which saturates	2.5g
Salt	0.1g
Fibre	1g

Stem ginger biscuits

With little chunks of stem ginger baked into them, these spicy biscuits are very moreish!

INGREDIENTS

3 balls of preserved stem ginger, finely chopped, and 1 tbsp syrup from the jar

115g (4oz) unsalted butter, softened, plus extra for greasing

85g (3oz) light muscovado sugar

1 egg

175g (6oz) self-raising flour

60g (2oz) plain flour, plus extra for dusting

1 tsp ground ginger

pinch of salt

MAKES 24   **PREP** 10 MINS    **COOK** 15 MINS

1 Preheat the oven to 190°C (375°F/Gas 5). Lightly grease 2 baking sheets and line with baking parchment.

2 Place the butter, sugar, and ginger syrup in a large bowl and cream together using an electric whisk, until light and fluffy. Thoroughly whisk in the eggs. Sift over the flours, ground ginger, and salt, then fold into the mixture along with the chopped stem ginger.

3 Heap 24 dessertspoonfuls of the mixture onto the prepared baking sheets. Place the dollops well apart as they will spread during baking. Flatten the dollops with your fingertips; if the mixture is too sticky, then dust your fingers with flour before flattening.

4 Bake for 15 minutes until golden. Cool for 5 minutes on the baking sheets and, using a palette knife, transfer to a wire rack and leave to cool completely. Store in an airtight container for up to 3 days.

Nutrition data per serving

Energy	93kcals/391kJ
Carbohydrate	12g
of which sugar	5g
Fat	4g
of which saturates	2.5g
Salt	trace
Fibre	0.4g

Fruit and seed soda bread

A tasty loaf that helps you get more fruit into your diet.

INGREDIENTS

sunflower oil, for greasing
50g (1³/₄oz) mixed dried fruit
175g (6oz) wholemeal flour
1 tbsp bicarbonate of soda
60g (2oz) sunflower seeds
150g pot plain yogurt

MAKES 1 LOAF   **PREP** 10 MINS   **COOK** 20-25 MINS

1 Preheat the oven to 180°C (350°F/Gas 4). Lightly grease a 450g (1lb) loaf tin. Place the dried fruit in a heatproof bowl, pour over 100ml (3½fl oz) boiling water, and set aside for 10 minutes.

2 Mix the flour, bicarbonate of soda, and seeds in a large bowl. Stir in the fruit in its water and the yogurt.

3 Pour the mixture into the prepared tin and bake for 20–25 minutes or until firm. Allow to cool for 10 minutes before slicing.

Nutrition data per serving	
Energy	129kcals/539kJ
Carbohydrate	9g
of which sugar	2g
Fat	3g
of which saturates	0.7g
Salt	0.3g
Fibre	2g

Roasted figs with citrus crème fraîche

A simple dish with "wow factor" flavour.
Figs are a good source of iron.

INGREDIENTS

8 fresh figs, stalks snipped

juice of 2 oranges

2 tsp sucralose
    sweetener (Splenda)

pinch of ground cinnamon

150g (5¹/₂oz) low-fat
    crème fraîche

juice and zest of ¹/₂ lime

SERVES 4   **PREP** 5 MINS   **COOK** 20 MINS

1 Preheat the oven to 200°C (400°F/Gas 6). Make a cross at the top of each fig and gently squeeze the fruit apart a little. Place the figs in an ovenproof dish.

2 Pour in the orange juice, and sprinkle with the sweetener and cinnamon. Put in the oven to cook for about 15 minutes until the figs have softened and are beginning to caramelize.

3 Mix the crème fraîche with the lime juice and zest, and spoon it over the figs in the dish. Serve immediately.

Cook's Tip: For a special occasion, you could drizzle a tiny amount of cassis over the figs before roasting.

Nutrition data per serving

Energy	111kcals/467kJ
Carbohydrate	13g
of which sugar	12g
Fat	6g
of which saturates	4g
Salt	trace
Fibre	1g

Lemon cheesecake

This low-fat version of a traditional baked cheesecake
is just as full of creamy flavour.

INGREDIENTS

100g (3¹/₂oz) sucralose
    sweetener (Splenda)
juice of 2 lemons and zest
    of 3 lemons
4 eggs, separated
150g (5¹/₂oz) low-fat
    cream cheese
200g (7oz) quark cheese
50g (1³/₄oz) sultanas
2 tbsp plain flour
butter for greasing

SERVES 8   **PREP** 5 MINS    **COOK** 50 MINS

1 Preheat the oven to 170°C (340°F/Gas 3¹/₂). In a large bowl, dissolve the sweetener in the lemon juice, then add the egg yolks and whisk until pale and thick. Add the cream cheese and quark and beat until smooth.

2 Empty the lemon juice and zest into the cream cheese mixture, then add the sultanas. Stir to mix. Sprinkle the flour over the mixture and fold it in gently. In a clean bowl, using a clean whisk, whisk the egg whites until stiff, then fold into the cheesecake mixture.

3 Spoon the mixture into a deep, round, 20cm (8in) springform cake tin, greased and lined with greaseproof paper. Bake in the oven for 45–50 minutes or until golden and almost set; it should still wobble slightly in the centre. Leave to cool in the oven with the door open (this should prevent it from cracking too much).

4 Once cooled, run a knife around the edge of tin, release the sides and carefully remove the cheesecake.

Nutrition data per serving

Energy	121kcals/509kJ
Carbohydrate	9g
of which sugar	6g
Fat	5.5g
of which saturates	2g
Salt	0.1g
Fibre	0.3g

Acknowledgments

The Diabetes Cooking Book (2010) **Authors** Fiona Hunter and Heather Whinney; **Art director** Luis Peral; **Food stylist** Cara Hobday; **Prop stylist** Victoria Allen; **Home economists** Richard Harris, Emily Shardlow, and Rachel Wood; **Out-of-house editors** Helena Caldon and Fiona Corbridge; **Project editors** Robert Sharman and Saloni Talwar; **Designers** Katherine Raj and Devika Dwarkadas; **Senior creative art editor** Caroline de Souza.

The Gluten-Free Cookbook (2012) **Authors** Fiona Hunter, Jane Lawrie, and Heather Whinney; **Recipe editors** Jane Bamforth and Holly Kyte; **Recipe testers** Rebecca Blackstone, Anna Burges-Lumsden, Amy Carter, Jan Fullwood, Laura Fyfe, Katy Greenwood, Anne Harnan, Catherine Rose, and Rachel Wood; **Food stylists** Marie-Ange Lapierre and Emily Jonzen; **Hand model** Danaya Bunnag; **Senior editors** Alastair Laing and Chitra Subramanyam; **Project art editors** Katherine Raj, Prashant Kumar, and Anamica Roy.

Family Kitchen Cookbook (2013) **Author** Caroline Bretherton; **Nutritionist** Fiona Hunter; **New photography** Lis Parsons, William Reavell, and Stuart West; **Photography art direction** Susan Downing, Geoff Fennell, Lisa Pettibone, and Penny Stock; **Food styling** Emma-Jane Frost, Paul Jackman, Jane Lawrie, Rosie Reynolds, and Penny Stephens; **Prop styling** Susan Downing, Liz Hippisley, and Wei Tang; **Photography shoot manager** Anne Fisher; **Consultant for Babies and Toddlers chapter** Rosan Meyer; **Recipe testers** Jane Bamforth, Ramona Andrews, Anna Burges-Lumsden, Amy Carter, Sue Davie, Francesca Dennis, Hulya Erdal, Georgina Fuggle, Jan Fullwood, Anne Harnan, Richard Harris, Sue Harris, Jo Kerr, Sarah King, Emma Lahaye, Bren Parkins-Knight, Ann Reynolds, Cathy Seward, Rachel Wood, and Amanda Wright; **Senior editors** Scarlett O'Hara and Dorothy Kikon; **Senior art editors** Sara Robin and Ivy Roy; **Editors** Lucy Bannell.

Family Nutrition (2014) **Author** Jane Clarke; **Recipe consultant** Caroline Bretherton; **Nutritionist** Fiona Hunter; **Recipe tester** Katy Greenwood; **Prop stylist** Isabel de Cordova; **Food stylist** Jane Lawrie; **New photography** William Reavell; **Senior editors** Camilla Hallinan and Ira Sharma; **Project art editor** Katherine Raj and Simran Kaur; **Editors** Carolyn Humphries and Diana Vowles; **Designers** Mandy Earey, Saskia Janssen, and Simon Murrell.